The Kraut

The Kraut:
On Being German after 1940

*Hurlothrumbo: An opera where events are connected
more by hilarity than design and played out sometimes
in one key, sometimes in another, sometimes fiddling,
sometimes dancing, and sometimes walking on stilts.*

by
Erik Jürgen-Karl Dietrich

Acknowledgements

Captain Brayton Harris, USN. Forty years of absolute trust, affection, encouragement, and support. I never had a better skipper; no one has.

Tim Foote who told me to get this thing written. "Before you're fifty," he said. That was twenty-five years ago.

Lincoln Paine, the most gifted maritime historian of our age, who motivated me to actually sit down and begin. He then became the sort of editor who actually understands what he's reading. He clarified, questioned sequences, identified errors, and properly raised his eyebrows at my tendency for over-the-top conservative polemics. I am still stunned by the magnitude of his gift to me.

Paul Ridgway, FRGS, FRIN, a writer, historian, and much respected colleague of many years standing with whom I had the privilege of serving on the board of the World Ship Trust.

Bill Truckey, my patient brother-in-law who never complained at yet another ambush of a draft chapter. We may have been on opposite sides at our beginnings but there's not a historical personality in these pages he doesn't recognize.

Karen Truckey, my beloved niece, who designs great book covers.

And Sarah Truckey, who cheered us to continue when illness became a distraction.

Dedication

In cheerful gratitude to:

Roberta Lucile Truckey who loves me to the moon and back;
Dayna Luann Diamond, Maxwell Scott McNamara, Moxie Rhedyn Rotter my grandchildren, and Michael Greenstein, whom we never forgot. This narrative was written with you in mind.

The sons and daughters who give my life definition and purpose, Lillian Elisabeth Diamond, Monique Marie Travelstead, Theodore Andrew Travelstead, Kimberly Berryman Rotter, Stefanie Ilana Berryman English, Mike Berryman, and the children who came to us by marriage whom we embrace just the same, Julie Wright, Anthony Michael Rotter, Michael Joseph English.

Judith Susan Milner Jennings and Jerome "Jerry" Jennings and Jimmy and Dawn Travelstead for helping to make a complete family out of fragments. Chester Travelstead, who added us to his family tree and Marita, his wife, who remembered my name when she was already deep into Alzheimer's. Coleman Travelstead and his wife, Brookes, because much of a family's happiness pivots on the kindness of an uncle.

Florence Truckey whose calm acceptance meant the world to me,

and

the unknown immigration official at the US Embassy in London, who in September 1957 took seriously a skinny, uncredentialed seventeen-year-old asking to come to America unaccompanied, and forever

Thank you.

CONTENTS

Prologue and Summary

Wake and start up. [Stage directions to sleeping characters.]
—*A Midsummer Night's Dream,* 4

I've been married for more than half a hundred years, since I was twenty-one. Most of my life. Sixteen years the first time. Thirty-five years and counting on the second attempt, launched with scant hope of success but still, astonishingly, wondrously successful. Palmer Larson, an Army chum who served in the same military police battalion as I did, was a seventy-five-year old bachelor farmer living with his seventy-year old brother, also a bachelor farmer, on a small farm ninety miles north of Des Moines, Iowa, where he was born and lived all of his life except for the short stint in uniform. He needed a knee replaced and reported into the local hospital where the receptionist asked a lot of questions. My stepson Ted could have written this anecdote into one of his Hollywood scripts.

Palmer recounted, "When you're a bachelor you have to go around and around with married women who don't understand. The receptionist at the hospital where I was an outpatient filled out a form on my life history. When I got done she had me read it over, and she had me down as married. I said 'Whoa!' I told her I was a bachelor. She said divorced? I told her never married. She said I look married. I told her it must be the arthritis."

When our children got old enough to focus on my accented English and ask questions, I began to tell them about my past. Briefly. In fits and starts to suit the moment. Professionally unemployed and paid to stay home, the writing down of things came late, well along in middle age. I work at glacial speed. My tempo is like that of the poet Richard Wilbur, who said of himself, "Composition for me is, externally at least, scarcely distinguishable from catatonia." I wanted to collect the anecdotes before old age induced apathy, or senility had leached out means and will. Personal vignettes seem to gain momentum after Social Security kicks in, perhaps because that's when the long ago is more sharply remembered than whatever it was that we had for dinner last night. There are grandchildren now.

The metaphysical tissue that connects either end of seventy-five years is an identity dilemma that formed in the first seventeen years as I lived them during the 1940s and 1950s in Germany and in Wales and England. The problem is peculiar to the twentieth century, particularly for the cohort of Germans who experienced the war. An obsession to remember did not have the same force after I came to America. I had to wait to become an old man for that.

And so did the need to rehabilitate the name on my birth certificate, now on the title page of this book. It is the name that was taken from me for well-intentioned but misguided reasons after the war. Berryman never felt right. The fit was off. That's not who I am. I'm a German-American immigrant with a proper German name, and I'd just as soon everybody know it when the house lights dim and the reel starts to flicker on the screen.

First came elopement to Yonkers, New York, and marriage in the spring of 1962 to Judith Susan Milner, a witty, spirited, Brooklyn Jewish girl with a flawless complexion. We met in Greenwich Village on my first trip to New York City. I had volunteered to be a guinea pig at the Army's Chemical and Biological Center in Edgewood, Maryland. This got me out of Ft. Hood, Texas. Judy gave me the linear clarity of Judaism, three capable children—all girls: Lillian, 1964; Kimberly, 1969; and Stefanie, 1970—and a gloriously kind and bounteous father-in-law whose compassion shaped our life. Irving Milner authored the introductory lines of what could have become the greatest of all American detective novels: "Johnny Spain was a bum. His brother helped him. At night they flew pigeons off the roof."

In life-long rebellion against his Orthodox father's severity, Irv's gourmet BLTs and especially his high-end pork roasts became legendary. He was a large man, tall and well built. Looked a lot like Carl Reiner and had similar mannerisms and wit, and an impulse to zaniness. A gifted man, qualified attorney from Brooklyn Law, friend and confidant of movie pioneer Spyros Skouras. No pretensions. No grinding axes. Much too generous to his children. Irving Milner, born Manhattan, March 30, 1909, died far too young in Queens, New York, January 3, 1970, with a cigarette between his fingertips. He never got to hold Kim or Stefanie.

Marriage to his daughter ended in 1979, on Valentine's Day. What endures is memory of the bond's astonishing power at the start. Two very young people in a partnership that didn't have enough steam but who remained united over the fortunes of their children and grandchildren. It is a poverty when divorced couples forget their beginnings. Not like my father, who used a scissors to cut out my mother's image from every snapshot that had me in it. And my mother, who told me my father was killed in the war.

The US Army and the Vietnam War. Life on a querulous, late-1960s college campus. The 1970s as a lieutenant orbiting the secretary of the Navy in the Pentagon's E-Ring. Expeditions to the Falklands and North Sea in search of ghosts and shipwrecks. A second marriage in January 1980, although my personal calendar marks us as a permanent item on May 16, 1979, the day I left to find John Paul Jones's *Bonhomme Richard* in the North Sea. This time to a freckled Catholic girl of Irish-French-Swedish extraction, Roberta Lucille Truckey. The incomparable Bobbie, in whom humor, abundant common sense, and goodness tumble over themselves to find expression. She made us a life and a home. Bobbie brought two stepchildren, both artists: Monique, born 1966, and Theodore Travelstead, 1968. By sheer force of personality and the combined efforts of ex-spouses and former in-laws, the fragments became a family again in which the children grew up supportive of one another's endeavors and taking pleasure in each other's company, grandchildren are completely interchangeable, and the elder-elders sit down together to dinner.

The Kafkaesque Immigration and Naturalization Service of the 1990s. On the inside of the intelligence community, where secrets are a kind of intra-agency commodity. To retirement in 2003 and the rest of what went into fifty years are all an apostrophe to those nascent seventeen years.

Coming to America was the seminal event of my life. Mid-twenti-eth-century opinions lie here thick on the ground. I was a helicopter door gunner in Vietnam's Mekong Delta, my life in the Army and Navy, the university experience in the pitiable Age of Aquarius, federal government civil service, and all that transpired since I added my name to the US im-migration quota for Germans in 1957 feature, but none of it sits at center stage. My foundation was built on the formative years, perhaps as it is for all of us. Jesuits have a saying: "Give me the child until he is seven and I will give you the man." In truth, I am German to the marrow and as such it is Wagner's kettledrums filtered through delivery of Bulwer-Lytton's "dark and stormy night" that best fits as the first line of this narrative.

The play is now well along in its last act. The audience has started to rustle, sneak looks at the time, and glance about for the exits waiting for the last scene to wrap up what's played out with so much *Sturm und Drang* since the curtain rose, and go home. In the wings I hear Bobbie urge,

> Listen / Listen
> Listen to me
> Time
> It's time
> Ten years like
> Ten minutes ago,
> Don't do it
> Don't do it
> Don't do it
> Wait,
> Take time.
> Take it. Take it.
> Oh, hurry
> Take it
> No time, Know time
> It's about time now. Now
> Now is all
> There is to know
> Now.

The House of Schleswig-Holstein-Sonderburg-Glücksburg

When his disguise and he is parted,
tell me what a sprat you shall find him.
—*All's Well that Ends Well,*
3.6.106–107

On a golden afternoon in the millennial year, I was part of a contingent invited to Buckingham Palace for an awards ceremony. We were a scrum that included an admiral of the fleet, some knights, and a couple of lords. The World Ship Trust, on whose Council I served as trustee and adviser, was to present its Maritime Heritage Award for historic ship preservation to the British clipper ship *Cutty Sark*. By precedence, the award was made in the Trust's behalf by the head of state or someone of similar, national stature. Past presenters include President Reagan and several kings and queens of Asia and Europe, including the Queen of England. This time we got Prince Philip, who was the Trust's patron during the International Maritime Heritage Year, in 1991.

He is known less formally as "Phil the Greek," on account of his parents having been the former king and queen of the Hellenes. We were a familiar crowd and he was a relaxed host. He joked about his colorful alias during the reception.

Before going to the palace, Trust and *Cutty Sark* representatives lunched together deep underground in the Stafford Hotel's wine cellars, which are part of a subterranean tunnel system dating to the sixteenth century. The tunnels run extensively under London's streets. After the port was served, our French chairman rose and reminded us that it was one day and fifty-five years after the end of World War II. He spoke at some elaborate length about what a mighty struggle it had been in those dark days, and he eloquently thanked the English for their crucial support of France during the war.

Refills accompanied choruses of "here-here." Knuckles rapped linen-covered tabletops. We were a nicely oiled and mellow troop that ambled through the park to the big gilded palace gates. Past knots of gawping tourists who took our photograph, past the constable checking our names, and past bearskin-helmeted, scarlet-coated grenadiers who presented arms and came to boot-crashing, brain-jarring attention, on through a doorway at the front right-hand corner of the palace into a waiting room.

There was no sign of an electronic security check, nothing I could detect. Our chairman had his suitcase along because he was returning to Paris on the Eurostar from Waterloo immediately after the ceremony. No one asked to inspect the contents. If people were being watched it was all very discrete and unobtrusive. A young Guards officer met us. He was doing a couple of years with the Royal Household as an *aide-de-camp*; it wasn't career-enhancing military duty but it was interesting, he said. We liked him at once.

The officer led the way up a green-carpeted, winding staircase to a long corridor lined with portraits in ornate gilt frames. A thick red carpet tapered to a point on the far horizon. The perspective down the length of the palace was like looking through a telescope backwards. Midway down the corridor we turned left into a formal reception room decorated in what the eighteenth century called *chinoiserie*, surrounded by hand-painted silk wallpaper of mandarins and empresses and large Oriental porcelain vases. The andirons in the two fireplaces were dragons and pagodas. The chandelier was a vast frosted-glass contraption, hand-painted with flowers. Besides a couple of tables at either end of the room there was no other furniture. The impression was exotic formality and coldly impersonal.

This was the room behind the center balcony from which King George VI with his family along with Winston Churchill waved at the huge crowd outside on VE Day in 1945.

We were split into two groups, *Cutty Sark's* minders and the Trust—the Jets and the Sharks—at opposite ends of the room. The tea was weak, the biscuits so-so. The crockery elegantly translucent and served by liveried footmen wearing frock coats, trousers, and waistcoats all in black and sporting lots of oversized, bright brass buttons. Tweedledums and Tweedledees bearing trays. The cups bore an anchor motif in gold and green. Someone remembered the china as having previously been aboard the royal yacht *Britannia*.

The Prince entered the room without any especial announcement and we were all introduced, one after another in rows. Earlier, the aide gave us "The Form" of what to do on first meeting royalty. That this was no ordinary social was plain in the invitation, which said the event would be "in the presence of." We were going to meet an aura. But when he came to me I couldn't make my neck bend. My mouth would not form the words, "Your Royal Highness." I left Berlin for England at the age of seven and Liverpool for the US ten years later. I stuck with a plain "Sir," delivered eyeball-to-eyeball. No bow, no elevated address even on his turf. I had become just another garden-variety product of the American republic.

We shook hands and spoke. He kept one hand behind his back. His

Eye-to-eye with a German prince.

face was finely lined and ruddy and he cocked his head at an angle when he spoke. It was a face that had never seriously been refused anything it wanted in life. We were about the same height. Since I have a naval rank, conversation drifted to the war. At lunch my near neighbor, the master of the *Cutty Sark*, called a point of order to say that the war wasn't just an Anglo-French success, but an American victory also. I don't think the others were especially keen to acknowledge the United States, but they'd been summoned to the task and responded well enough. Everyone thanked me. Now, the Prince was saying thank you for America's assistance in winning that great conflict. I smiled politely. He reminisced about his destroyer service afloat at that time, more than half a century earlier. Our chairman said he was inside a Free French tank somewhere in Bavaria.

In the company of Prince Philip and an old French warrior, my own memory of how the Second World War ended did not fit the congratulatory mood. In any case, to suddenly pop out of hiding to reveal the German I am would have been a spoiler.

The Prince turned to meet the person next in line, a large and visibly nervous woman whose high-heeled curtsey caused her to totter alarmingly. The whole room tensed as her brightly, over-dressed body started to surrender to gravity, but she found her balance at the last moment and regained the vertical. The Prince left in the same quiet way in which he had come, thirty minutes later on the dot. We looked through the curtains at the statue of Victoria in the traffic circle outside, talked some more, finished our tea and biscuits, and drifted slowly out behind him. The towering golden gates opened once again, other tourists took photographs of us, and we were back in the park headed for a drink at the Stafford.

Not Bulwer-Lytton after all. My start can take its cue from Thomas Merton: Under a waning moon on the third day of August 1940, under the sign of the lion in a year of a great war upon a hill at St. Josef's Hospital in Berlin-Tempelhof nearing midnight, I was born to Ella von Wernen-Barbutzki and Karl Dietrich. The world was turning into a picture of Hell.

Kill 'em All

Besides, there is no king, be his cause
never so spotless, if it come to the arbitrament of
swords, can try it out with all unspotted soldiers.
Some, peradventure, have on them the guilt of
premeditated and contrived murder

—*Henry V,* 4.1. 212–216

My earliest memory of World War II is a nighttime bombing of Berlin when I was still young enough to be carried. A man had me in his arms as he ran, my mother in full trot beside him. The air was full of burning cinders, countless brightly glowing bits of fiery orange that swam and danced and whirled above and around us. My mother swatted the embers briskly when they landed on me. I howled not from fright but from her energetic whacks. Over a lifetime, I have come to believe that the deliberate targeting of Germany's urban residential areas belongs to a different chapter, same book, of the Holocaust.

There is no moral contrast between those who stuffed the bodies of murdered innocents into concentration camp crematoria, and those who consigned their living bodies directly into the furnace by incinerating them from the air. There is only a difference in the cut and color of the uniforms.

American as well as British flyers dropped their bombs on German cities. Americans aimed chiefly at strategic targets, and mostly in daylight attacks. The British came at night and introduced terror bombing specifically to destroy the morale of the people. Historian John Keegan characterizes the RAF's decision as having "descended to the enemy's level." What

I find galling is the solemn pomposity with which Britons, civilian as well as military, defend their wartime government's actions in this respect.

I want a collection of awards made to Bomber Command crews to piece out of them a Giacometti-like monument to contrast with the rigid figure of Arthur Harris outside his London church. I want to take all those Distinguished Flying Crosses and Distinguished Flying Medals, Pathfinder badges, Distinguished Service Orders, and whatnot baublery identified as belonging to Harris's crews and weld them into a distorted shape of people, mouths agape, glowing incandescent in the flames.

British historian Fred Taylor offered a sharply contrasting opinion when I sent him my Holocaust-Allied air forces equivalency assessment. "Hate mail," he said it was. For a February 2005 interview with *Der Spiegel* he opined, "There have been some calls in Germany for the day of the destruction of Dresden to be commemorated. *If that were just used to exemplify German suffering then it would be wrong.* [Italics added.] But as an example of what advanced industrial countries have to try to avoid in the future then it is a legitimate symbol."

Taylor tells Germans what history they are permitted to question, feel guilty about, or mourn. He is unaccustomed to contradiction by Germans. Anyway, he wrote to me, too many decades have passed since German civilians were immolated en masse. "Most people involved are dead and we shouldn't start pointing fingers except for in the case of the Holocaust." For Taylor, war criminals are indicted selectively. Crimes against humanity by other than Germans are irrelevant, inconceivable, or have an expiry date.

He concluded tartly, "Your equivalence of the bombing of Germany (presumably along with the German bombing of Britain, Holland, Russia and Poland and Yugoslavia) with the holocaust is . . . disgusting." I am to understand all bombing is equal. In Taylor's circle, the calibrated mass destruction by firestorm of Germany's residential areas was all about stopping the "killing of Jews and other races felt to be 'inferior' by Germans and others serving the Nazi state." Some of his best friends are German, he added.

Smugness on this scale can change weather patterns over Peoria.

Taylor's *casus belli* summation is manifestly, objectively untrue. Neither Britain nor the United States went to war for social justice. The Royal Air Force's Arthur Harris (his Stalinesque statue overlooks the Strand, outside St. Clement Danes) had as his personal goal the virtual annihilation of the German civilian population. Taylor is silent on Harris.

Harris tried mightily to eradicate Germany as a functioning, modern industrial nation by leaving just enough population and infrastructure for an agrarian state. Harris labeled precision bombing advocates as "panacea-mongers." German-born Lord Cherwell (Frederick Lindemann) lobbied for a vastly increased effort in urban saturation bombing. He expected Bomber Command to transform at least a third of the population of National Socialist Germany into refugees within about a year. His "de-housing" goal was aimed at the fifty-eight largest German cities and would, he promised, "break the spirit of the people." Annihilation of so many homes, he confidently said, would be the most difficult burden for the population to bear.

A German remembered: "The men hammered out chunks of the wall and we tested to see if the pram would pass through, and it did! We came out at the Stadtdeich but into a thundering, blazing hell. The streets were burning, the trees were burning and the tops of them were bent right down to the street, burning horses out of the 'Hertz' hauling-business ran past us, the air was burning, simply everything was burning! The hurricane was so strong, that we could scarcely breathe, and I still know today that I screamed, 'Don't fall down!' at my mother." And, "Women and children charred unrecognizable. Half charred bodies, of recognizable remains of people dead from a lack of oxygen. Brains poured out of temples that had been burst, bowels hung out from under the ribs. The death of these people must have been dreadful. The smallest children lay like roasted eels on the surface of the road; in death, their features still showing how they had suffered with their hands stretched out to protect themselves from the pitiless heat. I had no more tears."

Martin Middlebrook, who specialized in the war's bombing offensive, wrote that, "in some ways, area bombing was a three-year period of deceit practiced on the British public and on world opinion." The deceit, "lay in the concealment of the fact that the areas being most heavily bombed were nearly always either city centers or densely populated residential areas which rarely contained any industry."

Harris's regret was not getting the 4,000 heavy bombers he needed to destroy Germany end to end. His hatred had nothing to do with saving Jews. Harris's rage was genocidal and engineering his aerial Armageddon makes him a war criminal, as heinous as anyone or anything condemned at Nuremberg. Britain's Fred Taylors cannot escape their English, postwar schoolboy lessons left unexamined as adults. Fiercely defended, simplistic, and dishonest, propaganda-fed history is the consequence.

The late *Vanity Fair* journalist Christopher Hitchens belonged in the same mix. Bomb 'em all to kingdom come, as far as he was concerned. Hitchens approved the saturation bombing of German cities because, exactly Taylor's view, it punished the inhabitants for National Socialism's horrors. Richard Overy's *The Bombers and the Bombed* (2014) follows the British Air Ministry's painstaking research into making sure that German cities would be consumed by firestorms that sucked oxygen out of the air, killing tens of thousands. To reach its objective, the Ministry imported fire safety officials from the United States to advise on the optimum means of immolating private German houses. As one of a population of boys in the RAF/USAAC cross hairs of the time, is it disingenuous to ask what I was guilty of? The late Eric Markusen and David Knopf in their 1995 book, *The Holocaust and Strategic Bombing*, describe the Allied air campaign as genocide. Not the last word, certainly, but at least another puncture in the dying balloon of what passes as twentieth-century history for Taylor and his ilk in the British Isles.

We can make national judgments but not in one direction alone. Layers of complexity abound in the study of the origins of the twentieth century's world wars that have hardly been examined with anything approaching objective detachment, including the horror that became National Socialist Germany.

A hellish problem with attempting to challenge entrenched attitudes is that English friends no longer want to be friends. Keep quiet and go along or speak up and lose the hard-won status of being "the Good German." What to do? Wholesale condemnation of Germans induced in me one of the most protracted instances of Stockholm syndrome in psychiatric history, and arguably at least as personally affecting as anything undergone by the Manchurian Candidate. It would have gone easier if I had stayed and made my life in Germany. By leaving, the German war years became fixed in my memory like specks of pollen suspended in amber.

Simply, "I went to school in England. I am German" is an admission that was hard to make.

Announcement of Cardinal Ratzinger's election to the papacy brought an orgy of anti-German spite by British media aghast that a German had been chosen Pope. British tabloids as well as several of my Brit colleagues and their children at once pegged Benedict XVI as a National Socialist. Later, BBC coverage of the pope's visit to England was laced with footage of Hitler Youth parading swastika flags. The calumny cannot stop itself. Its reach is limitless. In 2011, Hitchens blamed Germany (the Kaiser this time, not Hitler) for Osama bin Laden, Islamic jihad, and the 9/11 attacks on New York City and the Pentagon (where my wife was working at the time, separated from the impact by a brand-new fire wall).

For over half a century in the English-speaking world, I hid behind the camouflage of an English name and the trace of an English accent. Colleagues with whom I worked closely had me down as a Brit. It was something I worked at, not always consciously especially, but silently and with persistence. "Where're you from, Eric?" "Oh, I grew up in England." Dodge, weave, obfuscate. The truth is, I am a Hun. Bosch. Jerry. Fritz. Herm. Kraut. Heinie. Squarehead and Nah-zee who has learnt something about blending with the furniture. Ducking for cover began soon after the twin-engine plane that brought us from Germany touched ground in the London suburb of Croydon in the late autumn of 1946. As much for self-protection as from the need for acceptance, it was drilled into me by my parents that Kraut was not something I should admit to, let alone wear on my sleeve. Seventy years later, the pretense has congealed inside me and needs to be exorcized—at least on the printed page.

The experience must be similar to that of a Marrano forcibly converted but who maintains his Jewish faith in secret. In fact, I wanted to be English, but it was hopeless. English culture does not allow for hyphenated converts. Alas, I knew I was German. I aspired to be the Lone Ranger but suspected all along that I was Tonto. I was both inside the circle of beleaguered wagons frantically reloading my Winchester, and outside riding rings on the attack with my feathers blowing in the wind. I wanted to be Sergeant Archibald Cutter but suspected I was nearer the confused little brown fellow in a turban and small loincloth, Gunga Din. In Britain I started a double life that continued until, roughly, my retirement in America sixty-plus years later.

The Duke of Edinburgh plays the same game but in superior disguise. Not "The Greek" at all. He is "Phil the German," of the House of Schleswig-Holstein-Sonderburg-Glücksburg. All Kraut, like me.

England, Hollywood, and Germany: History as Stereotype

> Were it not pity that this goodly boy
> Should lose his birthright by his father's fault?
> —*Henry VI*, Part 3, 2.2.34–35

The war and being German shaped much of who I am. So has America. The subtext of my story is that to be born German in the twentieth century came with a ton of baggage and to live in post-war England was like running a perpetual gauntlet.

Ordinary labels we expect as our natural inheritance got blurred. My name changed. "It will help you fit in," they said. I became Eric Berry-man, the German "k" softened to "c". When it occurred to me, I asked if there was a middle name. "Jürgen-Carl" was the response. I stuck them in, mostly in a quasi-Biblical fashion, as "JC." Sans hyphen. Berlin was censored as a point of origin. "When they ask where you're from, say Vi-enna." Austria got an early dispensation and membership in the victims' club. Austrians' spirited participation on the German side in the Second World War is all but forgotten. Boorish now to mention the *Anschluss*, or *Heim ins Reich*. Whither Matthäus Hetzenauer's 345 sniper kills, Walter Nowotny's 258 aerial victories, or the other million-plus Austrians who fought World War II in a German uniform?

With tongue planted firmly in cheek, people have said that the twen-tieth-century history of Austria is an attempt to convince the world that Beethoven was Austrian, Hitler a German. The Army and Navy Club in Washington, DC, displays a shadow box honoring "The Band of Brothers." Among the awards, a medal awarded by Austria inscribed "Austrian Liberation." The club's president, an Air Force general, doesn't see the problem. It can hardly get any more cynical than that.

My language changed. "Ach, du Gott!" got simplified to "Gorblimey." The oak tree replaced the linden as the symbolic roots of my national inheritance. All round me, everything German was reviled. The language itself was vilified as guttural and harsh. The public German face when it did not look like Hitler channeling Charlie Chaplin was scarred, wore a perpetual sneer, and had a monocle screwed into one eye. German heads were square and shrieked spit-flecked clichés: "Verboten!" "Schnell!" "Sieg Heil!" "Juden raus!" "Achtung minen!" "Hände hoch!" "Vie haf vays to make you talk."

Agatha Christie's *Seven Dials* mystery offers the pattern as I came to know it in my time. Written after the First World War, when German stereotypes were already firmly locked in the English perspective, the tremendous popularity of her books helped ensure that the anti-German trope became the exemplar for villainy. A kind of clean-shaven Snidely Whiplash in a short haircut.

> "Then there's a perfectly poisonous German chap called Herr Eberhard. . . . This man sucks his soup and eats peas with a KNIFE. Not only that, but the brute is always biting his finger-nails—positively gnaws at them."
> "Pretty foul."
> "Isn't it?"

Elsewhere in the same novel:

> He had, perhaps, a more soldierly bearing than most footmen and there was something a little odd about the shape of the back of his head. . . . She had a pencil in her hand and was idly tracing the name Bower over and over again. Sud-

denly an idea struck her and she stopped dead, staring at the word. Then she summoned Tredwell once more.

"Tredwell, how is the name Bower spellt?"

"B-A-U-E-R, my lady."

"That's not an English name."

"I believe he is of Swiss extraction, my lady."

"Oh! That's all, Tredwell, thank you."

"Swiss extraction? No. German! That martial carriage, that flat back to the head."

How does a flat-headed, soup-sucking, green pea vandal, and nail-biter roll his eyes in prose? Now, I see the humor. Then, not so much.

I wanted to assimilate. Desperately. The rub was England's not-always-impassive resistance to those who come "from away," to use an old Maine label for people not born there. Relentless censure of all things German turned me into a closet German in cavalry twill with an English façade and English pretensions. I thoroughly admired men who had been awarded the Victoria Cross and had done extraordinary deeds, but I was also a stealth admirer of *Panzergrenadiers, Gebirgsjäger* with their edelweiss insignia, of U-Boats and the bearded sailors who prowled under the sea in wolf packs, of *Luftwaffe* pilots, Stuka dive-bombers and Messerschmitt 109s.

The passing years have not altered the focus. I value my friendship with U-995's skipper, Hans-Georg Hess. His Knight's Cross hard-won. His character unimpeachable. Douglas Bader is admired but Erich Hartmann sits on a mountaintop. Captain "Johnnie" Walker, RN, was a driven sea warrior in the mode of Ahab and the White Whale, but *Kormoran's* skipper Theodor Detmers served in the Horatio Nelson mode. Erwin Rommel and Heinz Guderian, Gerd von Rundstedt and Fridolin von Senger und Etterlin are in my pantheon of heroes. "Panzer" Meyer and Michael Wittmann belong there, also. Names like theirs are remembered, if at all, by a cadre of old codgers and pedants, but always with respect.

Hans Georg Hess died quietly on Friday, March 28, 2008, at his home in Wunstorf-Idensen, near Hannover. He was born May 6, 1923, in Berlin. From October 8, 1944, to February 14, 1945, aboard U-995 in Arctic and adjacent waters he fired thirty-five torpedoes for ten ships sunk or damaged including two destroyers, five freighters, an escort of the *Atherstone* class, a cutter (where he rescued two young Russian seamen from winter waters), and an American Liberty ship, the 7,000-ton *Horace Bushnell*. At twenty-one years of age, Hess was one of the youngest commanding officers of a combat submarine in the German Navy and, in fact, one of the youngest submarine captains in naval history as well as the youngest German Navy recipient of the Knight's Cross. The courage, skill, and tenacity of the U-boat captains have no equal in submarine warfare.

After the war Hess made his life as an attorney. We collaborated in the making of a detailed cut-away model of U-995, and in the translation of a guest editorial I wrote (and he translated) about the nature of German wartime military service scrubbed of caricatures. One summer, he was at the Hannover railway station when Bobbie and I arrived, and took us home with him. His telephone calls sounded like the skipper on his 1MC, "H-G hier! Erik?!" He hated the answering machine.

In early January 2004, Hess telephoned to discuss a conversation he had with Gerd Thäter, a U-boat ace who survived the Battle of the Atlantic. Thäter lay dying and had telephoned to ask if Hess would write and deliver the eulogy at his funeral. He did not know how much more time he had left. He was taking care of details. On the phone, Hess explained that he wanted to use an incident when he was under Thäter's command and asked if I thought it was suitable. It was a rhetorical question, really. He just wanted to tell me that he was an eighteen-year old aboard U-466 when the boat came under fearful depth charge attack, which Thäter was attempting to dodge by diving ever deeper into the sea, perhaps deeper even than the builder's predicted crush depth. The hull of the submarine complained loudly under the terrible pressure.

"I was visibly afraid," Hess said. "When Thäter looked up and saw my white face he leaned over to me and quietly said, 'Don't be afraid, Hans-Georg. We can't fall lower than into the hands of God.' I calmed down at once." And into the hands of God we commend the soul of Hans-Georg Hess.

Tim Foote, senior editor at *Time* in its halcyon days and later, in retirement, editor of *Smithsonian* magazine, recalled a story "by a guy at Harvard whose father had a 60-foot yawl and just before we got into the war he, like some other deep-water sailors, was pressed into service by the Coast Guard as amateur scouts, so the story went, to patrol for U-boats off soundings, having been equipped with radio connections and (good grief!) a 30-cal. machine gun! One grey day he was cruising far out when this huge black vessel reared up out of the sea beside him, dripping and hellish dangerous looking. The captain (presumably) with a black hat and a beard looked down at him, picked up a bullhorn and roared 'Go Home!' Which he did."

Propaganda-fueled stereotypes and caricatures infect so much of what has been written, and written largely by Allied historians who continue to accuse all Germans—no exceptions—of being criminally responsible for all the horror, and who see little or no fault in themselves. That is how "Bomber" Harris can get his statue put up outside a house of worship, and why the RAF's policy of terror bombing continues to be "debated."

As one of the *Kriegskinder* (war children) whose childhood was dismembered by the consequences of the war, I claim for my family and others who served with decency and honor, who fought, suffered terribly, and died in the millions that their only crime is that they answered the call to duty. There was no choice. Dictatorships are inflexible things. Perhaps more to the point, people fight for their country. Not a comfortable fact, but true all the same. My father, Karl Friedrich Dietrich, was a *Luftwaffe* scientist who helped materially in delivering rockets that blew whopping great holes in London neighborhoods. An uncle served aboard *Kriegsmarine* U-boats. Joseph Ratzinger was a *Wehrmacht* private, and I happily tagged along behind my mother, a *Wehrmacht* field nurse tending "our boys." Apologies not required.

Also, a kind of spiritual exhaustion has set in. After wrestling to accommodate, rationalize, struggle with, and compartmentalize Germany and the Second World War, I conclude at the end of my life that I don't much care any more. The war is over and paid for, as much as anything of the kind can be paid for. Paid in military and civil tribunals and ad hoc drumhead justice. Paid on the gallows and by imprisonment. Paid in treasure. Paid in guilt and doubt and shame. But fully paid up it all is by the German nation and its people of whatever age. I should live long enough to see the Soviet legacy brought to justice and the same derision applied to those who wear enameled pins of Vladimir Lenin or Che in their lapels as is accorded to wearers of the swastika. Emblems that exactly equate.

A national reversal on such an epic scale affected my identity and deepened as I integrated into the Anglo culture. I became my own *doppelgänger*. Even in America. Socially, it was too wearying to have to dive into tedious personal explanations when introductions were being made. "Yes, I went to a private school in Stroud. That's in Gloucestershire. You know, the Cotswolds."

We got opprobrium as an inheritance, my band of *Kriegskinder* and I, as well as the next several generations to follow. There is slim sign of a letup. The postwar years levied a relentless mortification on Germans and not least by Germans themselves. They crucified the writer Heinrich Böll and made a shambles out of novelist Günther Grass. A cocktail of his seventeen-year old gullibility and National Socialist cynicism got him to volunteer for the SS just as the war was ending. The actor Horst Tappert was outed, pilloried, and banished for having been a nineteen-year-old SS *Panzergrenadier*.

My mother's godson, Kurt Sydow, was all of fifteen years old when he faced the same kind of induction panel. "Tell us what you want," they bellowed. "*Infanterie, Flak, oder SS?*" Kurt blinked. Paused. "*Die Kriegsmarine,*" he stammered. It brought down the house. Fully aware that a boy in uniform had no chance of surviving what was left of German resistance, his mother pretended to break his arm and paraded him and his new, white plaster cast through their small town. The induction notice was suspended. If found out, she would have been hung. Publicly. From a lamppost.

The morbid, abiding, collective guilt that keeps postwar Germany confused and chained is as irrational as it is reprehensible. Absurdities abound: the miasma of discord that came from naming *Bundesmarine* warships *Luetjens, Moelders*, and *Rommel*. (I would like to see *Theodore Detmers, Erich Hartmann*, and *H-G Hess* added to the list). The juggernaut of hysterics by foreign media and Germans alike that rolled over Pope Benedict for being drafted into military service. The nonsense that labels U-995 in Laboe a "technical museum" instead of the remarkable example of a warship that she is. And now that Germany contributes forces in support of Allied military missions in hostile engagements, I would enthusiastically back the return of traditional German military decorations: the black Wound Badge, two classes of Iron Cross, and the Pour le Mérite for extraordinary heroism.

When Prussia's educational system was a model of achievement, when the quality and abundance of German art, music, literature, philosophy, and social organization illuminated the world, there was universal approbation of things German. The twentieth century did not obliterate these historic achievements or erase German strength of character, not even in the face of the judgment at Nuremberg after 1945. The years have imposed a relentless, endless abasement on Germans by outsiders with agendas of their own, as well as by Germans themselves who will not distinguish between objective truth and propagandistic fiction. The great secret is that the same brush does not tar all Germans who served in the Second World War, not even most Germans. If Germans are waiting for absolution from the outside world they wait without hope. This job they must do for themselves.

History is not black and white and Germany is badly overdue for a manifesto entitled *Vae Victis* that will probe the limits of abasement by a beaten people.

Mind, seventy years or so may have softened the edges here and there. The bite remains:

Chancellor Angela Merkel arrives at passport control at a Paris airport.

"Nationality?" asks the immigration officer.

"German," she replies.

"Occupation?" the officer asks.

"No, just here for a few days."

Blend In and Repeat the Words

The actors are at hand, and, by their show,
You shall know all that you are like to know.

—*A Midsummer Night's Dream*, 5.1.122–23

Films gave the identity crisis an edge. It was James Mason I wanted to be in 1953 when he played Erwin Rommel in *The Desert Rats,* and not the Scottish commando Richard Burton who opposed him. I told no one. At fourteen, I thrilled with everyone else watching *The Dam Busters* when Mike Todd as Guy Gibson, VC, DSO and Bar, DFC and Bar, jockeyed his cargo of barrel bombs on the raid to destroy the Möhner Dam. I was right there in the cockpit, tense but resolute, bulling my way to the target through a wall of pounding flack. I happily wore the sky blue Senior Scout troop patch that was designed to honor Gibson and his men in the burst of publicity that followed the film. We loudly hummed the theme music at one another as we bent low over the handlebars of our Lancaster bombers, pedaling like mad to deliver the payload 500 feet above the objective. It scarcely crossed my mind that I had been the target.

We did not disappoint Trevor Howard when the sentry under his coalscuttle helmet was about to be knifed by a stealthy Cockleshell hero. I secretly wanted to whisper "Psst! Look behind you!" but understood why he had to die. Years on, standing my first guard duty at night with a US infantry division in some forlorn region of German rocks and shrubbery near Grafenwöhr, memory of the moonlit movie killing came back to give me a turn or two. I admired immensely Marlon Brando as Lieutenant Christian

Diestl in *The Young Lions*, the first postwar film to portray a decorated German infantry officer with a pinch of sympathy. What a relief to see someone more like men I knew, and not the caricatures I had come to expect.

Diestl's characterization of a conflicted German soldier became a standard cliché that lives on like some ghastly thing from *Night of the Living Dead*. In recent times, Nick Stafford's technical marvel *War Horse*, about World War I, is historically coherent through Act One. But Stafford is English and incapable of transcending his schoolboy indoctrination. In his view British soldiers, decent to a man, serve a noble cause. Germans are all automatons on the dark side. Sense and history collapse after the intermission, when the central German soldier—for whom we are cued to feel a scrap of sympathy—acts out the cod's wallop of an agonized, politically misguided, post-World War II "good German soldier" in his moment of moral epiphany. All of it in a parody of German accent that would give Erich von Stroheim a facial tic and make Marlene Dietrich collapse with laughter.

War Horse is set in World War I, when the Red Baron's chivalry defined gallantry in air combat and Arnauld de la Perière's U-Boat exploits entered submarine warfare history books. But in Great Britain and Hollywood, Germans are all either villains or dupes. English novelist Martin Amis's 2014 novel *The Zone of Interest* ushers an entire people, past, present, and future, all ages and genders to damnation: "The German is not something supernatural, but neither is he something human. He is not the Devil. He is Death." Lurid, certainly (the scene takes place in Auschwitz) but trite, wearisome bunk just the same, and written with a film script contract in mind.

England generally and Hollywood in particular has traduced Germans for a century. Paul Bäumer's character and those of his chums in the American-made film version of *All Quiet on the Western Front* was not long remembered and never repeated. The inherent decency of the fictional Rittmeister (riding master) von Rauffenstein in Jean Renoir's

Grand Illusion vanished from portrayals of German soldiers. No conversation in Britain can start with Germany as its subject and not end with Hitler, someone said. German soldiers are all bad, incapable of goodness, generosity of spirit, or heroism. As the new century ticks along, not much has changed. People hang on to their clichés with near-desperation. Speaking of the *Wehrmacht's* highly effective small-unit tactics, a historian at the Imperial War Museum in London not long ago told me, "Well, of course they were outstanding. Who wouldn't be when there's someone at your back ready to shoot you down if you fail to obey orders?"

Auschwitz sealed the perception of Germans as villains as completely as any Cretaceous beetle embalmed in resin, as it was bound to do. The result is seventy years of the cinema's greatest generation's dirty dozen's inglourious basterds toiling on the longest day to cross a bridge too far to save Private Ryan and bring him home on the *Memphis Belle* reading Schindler's list.

Without Treblinka, Sobibor, Auschwitz, and the rest, the historical Hitler by now would have shrunk to the size of an operatic grotesque, one among many similar strutting malignancies in Europe's age-long experience of martial ambition, conquest, and savagery. Like the Kaiser in his handlebar mustache, a ridiculous figure. In both world wars, America felt no compulsion to charge into Europe's mess. It took years and assorted triggers to engage. Liberating oppressed minorities did not figure. *Herrenvolk* and anti-Semitism provoked weak reaction among all but a few Americans. Wither the steamship *St. Louis's* cargo of doomed Jewish refugees seeking asylum in a US port? "See," National Socialists gloated when the ship was forced to return to Europe, "no one wants them." And they were correct.

Britain went to war in 1939 because of Hitler's raw belligerence and treaty betrayals, not because of evils being done to Jews. The United States entered the Second World War only after Japanese bombs came down the stacks of the Pacific Fleet anchored at Pearl Harbor, two-plus years after the show began in Europe. Anti-Semitism has percolated in Britain at all levels of society, just as it has—and continues amain today—elsewhere in Europe and North America. British anti-Semitism is more covert and polished, that's all.

Only years later, when the shooting had all but stopped and news-reels began to flicker their horrific images, did Auschwitz frame the Allied cause, giving it resonance and purpose. Without journalists and their cameras, atrocities in the twentieth century by Ottoman Turks, the Soviets, and Mao's Red Brigade tyranny have no persuasive force or credibility. The accused make threats and deliver angry denials. Without the final solution, World War Two's origins would be as opaque today as the mass burning of the Armenian population of an entire village near Muş, Turkey. Or the Treaty of Locarno.

Genuine *Wehrmacht* joke: Two soldiers are in their foxhole looking at a world atlas together. One of them sticks his finger on a spot on the map and says, "That's Germany." "No," his companion smiles, "that's the United States of America." The map holder puts his finger on the map a second time, "Oh, then this is Germany." His buddy replies, "No, that's Russia." Once more the soldier points at a place on the map and says, "This is Germany!" "Yes," his companion tells him, "That's Germany." The first soldier suddenly looks very thoughtful and asks, "Does Hitler know that?"

The origins of the Second World War are not black and white. They are smudged-charcoal and dirty grey.

Of Those Who Claim Us

We are their parents and original.

—A Midsummer Night's Dream, 2.1.120

A dozen years my mother's senior, my father was an engineer and metallurgist in the *Vergeltungswaffe* program, the V-1 "buzz bomb" and its supersonic but equally imprecise successor, the V-2. *Vergeltungswaffe* means retribution weapon. The two Vs were warfare's first long-range missiles. He worked at a place with a name only Germans can love, the *Institut für Ballistik und technische Physik der technischen Akademie der Luftwaffe*, in Berlin-Gatow. TAL, for short, was a preeminent research facility and my father was so proud to be on its staff that he kept his government-issued identification credentials all his life. I found them among his papers. Matted and framed, the typed, stamped remnant hangs on my study wall. The initials TAL just barely visible in faded ink.

He ranked as a *Luftwaffe* major. The job conveyed prestige and allowed him priority travel on leave. At TAL, he befriended Robert Biberti, the basso of the incomparable Comedian Harmonists. One of their acts uses only voices to mimic the sound of musical instruments, "Creole Love Song." Pure joy. When we share in the music that quickened the pulse of our parents we know them better, if only for a moment. Biberti was drafted into Berlin's Air Raid Warning Central (*Luftschutzwarnzentrale*). He probably manned a post near the TAL lab, somewhere. Biberti wasn't a Jew.

Most of the rest of the troupe was Jewish or married to a Jew, which was almost as damning. Their act was shut down a few months after Hitler came to power. Chagall, Mendelssohn, pop harmonizers in an American jazz mode, the incomparable Richard Tauber, nothing and no one who gave sound and light and beauty was spared destruction if "Jew" could be attached to them in some way. Bewildering, incomprehensible stupidity spiced with homicidal savagery. I have ever been astonished at National Socialism's obtuseness, never mind its barbarism.

My father's überboss, Wernher von Braun, was commissioned *Sturmbannführer* in the SS, equivalent to major but with more glitz by the lights of the time. Braun surrendered to a welcoming US Army. His knowledge was invaluable and he was eagerly fêted by his captors, politics be damned. Both men were Party members, National Socialists. Each of them dutifully concluded official correspondence with the customary flourish "Heil Hitler." My father's surviving business letters do not include the exclamation mark, as in "Heil Hitler!" the usual form for those possessed of heightened *Führer* zeal. However small in detail, I want the omission to be a positive sign in a nation that had been fearfully corrupted by its monstrous government.

It was not the old, creased brown cloth ID card with its eagle and swastika stamps that stopped my heart. It was his photograph. The face on that ancient document was exactly as I remembered him the last time we saw one another in 1944. I was a staffer in the Pentagon when the State Department package arrived with its fatter-than-expected contents of document copies, among them his identification card. Half a century had come and gone but the shock of instant recognition took my breath away. We had seen one another often after 1955 and the chance discovery that he was alive. But the old ID photo made me four years old again, and he was at the end of the road again, coming in my direction. My heart used to outrace my feet when I saw him come down the dusty village road in Langenbrück, Upper Silesia, where I had been sent for safety from the bombing of Berlin. Time left me the memory of his face as it was, when I was a child. A glimpse of his silhouette at the foot of Maple Street in Cape Story by the Sea would move me just as wildly today.

We were separated by parental ill will, my mother's doing. These two

My father's TAL identification card. The face on that ancient document was exactly as I remembered him, from 1944.

people were polar opposites politically, by instinct, taste, and training. I had him from 1940 to about 1944. The war's end was exploited in some way to facilitate the closure of their relationship. Contact between them stopped altogether. He was dead, my mother told me. Killed. Gone. I wouldn't be seeing him again. The explanations were always vague, insubstantial, but five- and six-year-olds don't analyze in depth. The immediacy of even the sharpest memory softens around the edges. Questions became infrequent. Answers more oblique. John Berryman, Kurt Hennig, my Aunt Tulla, and my grandparents, everyone had the secret but no one said anything. Out of respect—or fear—of my mother. I think of their silence as a conspiracy and a betrayal.

Killed in the war, she said. In fact, my parents separated or divorced or never divorced and she just left to make another life. I never knew. He was captured sometime between January and March 1945. How much time he spent in a POW cage is unknown, but it was probably not much more than a year. (My half-brother was born on May 25, 1949.) Uniforms had a certain currency as the country collapsed.

An SS uniform was likely to get the wearer shot outright. But my father had a relatively benign military affiliation and officer's rank, and my notion is that he was taken prisoner as a *Luftwaffe* major. I have a single anecdote of his time as a POW. A guard saw him reach for a cigarette stub on the ground and stepped on his hand. As the boot ground his fingers into the dirt my father thought, "Of all the humiliations I don't have to invite this one," and never smoked again. The Soviets had an interest in him and for years after the war he feared being carted off for involuntary servitude in Russia's missile program. When US forces discovered his occupation, he was asked about coming to America to join the missile program. He declined. He did not return to postwar Berlin to live with his parents because the Russians made themselves notorious with their kidnappings.

"Killed in the war" rooted in my mind ever after. It is what I usually answer when people ask about my past. I think I want them to know that my father fought for his country (his country, not Hitler) and that I lost him not by some prosaic administrative action or parental pique but by sacrifice. It is a madness.

My German tenure ended in late 1947 when the England saga began.

I knew my father only briefly in fits and starts whenever the war let him come to visit. I adored him and his memory stuck, as it must in all small boys of similar circumstances. Details follow later in these pages, but I found him again when I was in my teens. Later, in 1966, after graduating from Hofstra University and before taking up a graduate assistantship at the University of New Mexico, we visited him in his home in Wernau. He embraced Judy and his granddaughter, Lilly, as did Ruth—my father's second wife and thus my stepmother—and my brother. Years later, when I told my brother about the State Department's dossier, we decided that there was little there, there. Membership was good for his career. I will never know how caught up he was with the pathology of his time, but there was no whisper of it in his interaction with me. The only badge I wanted from him was his NSDAP lapel badge (which I promptly lost) when he came on leave one day. He handed it over without an editorial. Jews who lived in the basement of his parent's house were asked to leave when things got especially dangerous, he told me. They were not denounced. Just told to go away. What would I have done in such a hideous time? I hope at least as much. What is unassailably true is that he was my father and that I loved him. Love him, still.

Family, like politics, is local.

So don't wave his party membership in my face or tsk-tsk about "Doodlebugs" (which he capably helped to assemble and arm) ambushing unsuspecting Londoners, and especially don't trot out some vapid inanity about "the German character."

His *National Sozialistische Deutsche Arbeiterpartei* (NSDAP, abbreviated and pronounced *Nazi*) number is 3899234 with an entry date of February 15, 1937. Membership qualified him for the archives of the State Department's Document Center in Berlin-Dahlem, where the records of all party members were kept under the control of US civil servants until the reunification of Germany in 1991. He was assigned to the *Ortsgruppe Lützow* in Berlin-Charlottenburg. The Center's files have him down as an applicant (*Anwärter*) with a motorized unit of the *Sturmabteilung* (SA), Hitler's private army in 1933. Nothing seems to have come of it. There was no issue of boots (*schwartz*) or *Shue mit gamaschen* (shoes with leggings) or service pants and shirt (*hell braun*, light brown), no service cap (*Wehrmachtnschnitt* IV) or "60mm-wide" *hell Havana braun* Sam Browne belt, or a *Pistole* PPK *mit Tasche*. The clerk drew a big X through all of that and endorsed my father's withdrawal on July 4, 1939.

My mother. So much of the war and the narrative that followed begins with, "My mother." How many more children would have been blown to bits, become frozen solids, made limbless, or withered to oblivion from starvation but for the universal German mother of that harrowing time. Dressed in tatters, hair tied up under a scarf, a child glued to her side, astonishingly resourceful, her face set with a mix of fear and defiance, the German mother of the age was as heroic and immortalized as any female in Euripides.

Mine had been a sales clerk with Karstadt in Berlin-Neukölln, the

LEFT: Ella von Wernen-Barbutzki, my mother. Born in Berlin, 1912, Died in Gloucester, England, 1972.

RIGHT: Buddenbrooks redux. L to R: Unidentified young man, my father Karl Friedrich Dietrich, engineer, born Sulzbach-Saar, December 3, 1901, died on April 24, 1970. My grandfather Friedrich Karl Dietrich, editor, born St. Ingbert/Saar-Pfalz on September 24, 1874, died on November 5, 1956. My paternal grandmother Wilhelmine Margarete Henrietta née-Munzlinger, born on January 4, 1876 in Sulzbach-Saar. Died in Berlin, March 5, 1956. PHOTO: Berlin, about 1934

department store on the corner of Hermannplatz and Urbanstraße. She'd been a hopeful at Ufa Studios in Babelsberg. Tending to diffidence and shy, she was thin, pretty, intelligent, and class-conscious. Her father was a "von," a military officer and member of the minor aristocracy in East Prussia. There was blue in our blood, I was often reminded. She was a stylish hanger-on in a social crowd of movie people and Luftwaffe officers mixed with personalities Christopher Isherwood would have recognized at once as Berliners. There was talk of acting ambitions.

Socially reticent or not, a series of breezy alliances led to lasting questions about my paternity. The lineup included Heinz Engel, a physician who peered intently at me when we met in 1949 on a visit to Berlin soon after the Airlift ended, and Kurt Hennig, her on-again, off-again lover from about 1928 when she was sixteen until his death in 1966. To this day, his

nephews remain half convinced that I am their relative. There was also an affair with Ernst Udet, the devil's general, with whom I share two ruinous traits: bouts of black depression and a penchant for tangled, destructive relationships with women. And Karl Friedrich Dietrich, who claimed me, and I him.

I was too small to remember much of our life in Berlin, but there are incidents that have passed into family lore. The prewar zoo's tropical exhibit had a small bridge that crossed directly over a crocodile pit where the creatures lolled around on the banks of an artificial stream. In my mother's telling, a narrow bridge with a single safety rail protected one side only. On an outing I got loose for a moment and drifted immediately towards the open side. On the instant I began to teeter off the bridge a soldier reached out, caught me by the scruff and held fast. In all her tellings my mother's demeanor and tone alternated between panic and irony. The soldier belonged to the most dreaded military organization in the world, the SS.

My paternal grandfather kept an allotment, one of the city-owned bits of land in Berlin that people leased sometimes for a lifetime, to use as a tiny urban, bucolic retreat. The custom continues to the present day. There was a garden shed with a small veranda for refreshments, a few vegetables. Most of all there were lots of flowers. The smell inside the shed was as intoxicating as the aroma and feel of the wet mud outside. My love of gardening comes from that place and time. Proust knew best why smells and sounds of long ago linger to old age.

Uniforms fascinate children everywhere in war, most especially the very young. For them it is life at an extended costume party. Evidently, I had an irresistible attraction for naval styles and colors and casually took off and put on sailors' hats from clothes racks in restaurants. Blue and gold and the deep blue sea are inborn traits, it seems. The only Christmas I remember in Berlin was in my grandfather's wonderfully spacious Wilhelmine apartment at Tempelhofer Berg 5, in Berlin-Tempelhof. I had an oil painting done of the house years on as a gift meant for my brother, but he died of sepsis and the painting came back. The artist did not include the

LEFT: Home. Templehofer Berg, 5. Machine gun bullets entered the room through the open window (third floor, left) when my grandfather, trying to save the house, put out the wrong flag during street fighting in the battle of Berlin, 1945.

RIGHT: The infamous 1940 Christmas gift when my grandfather gave me a toy helmet (the shiny bit at right, bottom).

flags that were flying from all the houses that day, including my grandfather's apartment window.

On a Christmas Eve in Berlin, I opened the door to my grandparents' formal living room, bright with the glow of a tree ablaze with real candles. Gifts scattered at its foot. There has not been a Christmas Eve since that came to being nearly as perfect. A photo survives of me sitting with a toy helmet, a gift from my grandfather, a veteran of the First World War. My mother thought the helmet was an insanely inappropriate gift. Like my *Waffen-SS* rescue at the Berlin zoo, the event was integrated into family folklore to be remembered and talked about ever after. I think I remember the helmet was made of cardboard and that I chewed off the color along the rim.

Of my mother's several liaisons, Kurt Hennig featured large. As a small boy, his parents nicknamed him "Tutschen," which roughly translates to Little Thing. Tutschen evolved into Tutta and that's what his nephews, Kurt and Horst Sydow, and I call him still, with a devotion undimmed by our accelerating decrepitude or his death half a century ago. Tutta was an ace auto mechanic with a clientele of high-ranking National Socialist officials who were dismayed when he was drafted (and issued his uniform in a cardboard box). They were about to lose their automotive genius and National Socialist officials liked their cars to run. The induction notice was quickly cancelled.

Tutta reached for his handkerchief and made a show of blowing his nose in crowds thrusting out their right arms shouting "Heil Hitler." Only slavering ardor or a runny nose escapes unwelcome attention and denunciation in a one-party state. In the chaotic last days of the battle of Berlin, Schultze-the-Milk was drafted into the *Volkssturm*, the last-ditch brigade of old men and boys as young as fourteen with orders to stop the Soviet Army. (The last of the fourteen-year-old boys, Reinhard Kunze, was released from a Russian POW camp in 2014, sixty-nine years after his capture.) Old, stout, and bald Schultze ran a bakery and milk shop on the ground floor of the building where Tutta lived and had his garage. Schultze believed what he was told about hopeless gestures, common sense, and lost wars and surrendered his rifle and his "uniform" of a helmet and an armband bearing the stenciled word, *Volkssturm*, or people's militia. Tutta buried Schultze's arsenal and regalia in the ruins of the Karstadt department store at the end of the street.

The barrel-organ man came round the tenement courtyards cranking tunes from the decorated wooden music box he pushed along. He wandered through the big arched doorway to stand surrounded on all sides by apartment windows. "Tutta's Oma," as I knew his mother and others rolled up a few pfennigs in a bit of newspaper to toss down. He tipped his hat at each donation. "Untern Linden," "Durch Berlin fließt immer noch die Spree" ("Through Berlin still flows the river Spree") the pipes wafted upwards.

All around, bombed-out buildings punctuated the landscape, mile after mile in every direction. In the last months and weeks of the war, Berlin had virtually no air defenses. The BBC would announce the next targets. "Tonight," they might say, "we will take out every garage in the city." RAF targeteers used the phone book to identify the repair shops, including Tutta's *Opel Reparaturwerkstat* on Urbanstraße, 88. He kept watch from the roof, spade in hand, as phosphorus bombs ignited a firestorm. When a burning canister landed on the roof, he used his shovel to toss it over the side to the street below. His mother watched from the living room balcony, windows wide open so as not to be hurt by flying glass. She refused to join her neighbors in the air raid shelter. "Es stinkt da unten," she said. It stinks down there. If this was her time, she wanted to see it coming.

We were a mutual adoration society, Tutta's mother and I. She accepted me as the only boy her son would ever produce, and when I left for America, this tiny woman bent by hardship and age, widowed for decades, wept with grief.

We were with my godmother Ille Nitke in her apartment in the Berlin suburb of Nikolassee on an evening when the sky started to be illuminated with searchlights. Ille was a small, slim woman with a sharp sense of expressionist absurdity. She was famous for being able to stand and, wearing trousers, successfully use the men's urinal in public toilets. Ille was the elegant *demi-monde* who had married a Red. He was conscripted by the *Wehrmacht* anyway, never mind the politics, and sent to the Eastern front to fight Russians. National Socialists could be droll. He came home with his health broken and died soon after the war was over.

Ille then took up with a rich man who owned a house near Wannsee with its own castle on the estate. Germans were made to surrender personal weaponry following the war. Taking the order literally, the man delivered his collection of antique pistols and swords in a wheelbarrow to the nearest police station. My mother and Ille smoked cigarettes in long amber-and-silver holders.

The two women were deep in conversation when an air raid started to play out over Mitte—the city center—several miles away. Hundreds of searchlights constantly crisscrossing gave the scene a kind of kaleidoscope effect that was utterly wonderful to see. 20th Century Fox was just as enthralled by these modern contraptions as I was and put them in their corporate logo. I had my seat in the large window, oblivious to what the two women behind me were doing or saying. The glass I had pressed my face against imploded in a shower of fragments that rained over me in a shower.

It happened so quickly that there was no time to be anything but astonished. The waves of concussion from the distant high explosives had shattered the window. My mother screamed. Both women ran to pull me away from the now gaping hole where the window had been. I came away unscathed. The US War Department rated searchlights like this at 990-million candlepower with a range in favorable weather of over 8,000 yards. Motoring at night, precisely the sort of edgy beam our less gracious side might want to engage when an oncoming car stubbornly won't dim its lights.

My other godmother (there were no godfathers) was Hanna Kuhn. Hanna married a Jew who fled National Socialist Germany for sanctuary in Argentina, leaving behind a son, Peter. Hanna adored Peter in the same happy, rapturous way that my daughters love their children. Peter brought home hungry tramps he wanted his mother to feed. I took his example and from time to time have brought home human strays, too. There was a sallow-faced woebegone on an Albuquerque street on Thanksgiving Day during the Hippy era. A Cuban, one of the Mariel boatlift refugees, waiting in the evening after work for a ride that never came. And a talented lunatic who wandered Portsmouth, New Hampshire, streets selling excellent little line drawings of the town's old buildings.

Peter's example, re-enforced by Orwell's *Down and Out in Paris and London*, taught me not to pass a beggar without giving something. Beggary is hard work and any mental reservation that might occur about being exploited is sanctimonious nonsense.

National Socialist racial laws labeled Peter Kuhn a *Mischling*, a hybridized German, or mongrel. With his Jewish father and Christian mother he fell into the category of those who were acceptable mutts. The war put him in *Panzers*—tanks. The 1950s were well along but Hanna held firm to the hope that Peter had survived and would come home. She met every POW troop train returning from Russia holding high a sign she made with her son's photograph much enlarged, his regiment and name in big block letters: "Have You Seen Him?" "Do You Know This Man?" But Peter never came back.

I met him once only that I remember, when he was home on leave. Radiantly handsome in his uniform he took my hand. We walked together along a country path outside Hamburg, on the grounds of Hanna's employer, Schwartzkopf. For reasons that can only be explained by Deity or a good psychiatrist, I have a notion that when my time comes to cross the bar it will be Peter Kuhn who comes to where I am, grins cheerfully, reaches out his hand and says, "Komm, junge. Wir gehen zusammen."

At about this time the *Mutter-und-Kind Verschickung* (mother-and-child evacuation) program let parents send their children to remote regions of the country, away from the major targets of Allied bombers. Thus, in 1943 I went to live in Langenbrück. The same region in which the English writer P. G. Wodehouse found himself locked in an internment camp. "How [did] I become an Internee?" Wodehouse asked. "Well, there are several methods. My own was to buy a villa in Le Touquet on the coast of France and stay there till the Germans came along. This is probably the best and simplest system. You buy the villa and the Germans do the rest." About his new surroundings he mused, "If this is Upper Silesia, what can Lower Silesia be like?" Mine was a similar experience. All I needed to do was wait for the RAF and the Germans did the rest.

In Langenbrück, we were assigned to an ethnic German household, Mutti Weil and her absolutely stunning daughter, Ludmilla. Ludmilla of

The incomparable Ludmilla Weil with her moonstruck minion. Langenbrück Krieigskinderheim, 1942.

the golden braids. Ludmilla, the protectress. Ludmilla of Perpetual Adoration whose aura I sought every waking hour. Just to look at her made me dopey with love. Langenbrück was a hamlet where horse-drawn farm carriages moved about on dirt roads. Vast open fields stretched around us, unconnected to the industrial-scale abattoir further east, Auschwitz. Our funerals were dignified events. Mourners followed a horse-drawn, enclosed hearse of solid black wood heavily carved and adorned with polished silver finials. Beveled, elaborately etched glass walls displayed the coffin aboard. A coachman dressed in black frock coat and top hat sat high up on a seat holding the reins.

In winter we crammed into horse-drawn sleighs, hands stuck deep inside muffs. In summer, we ran beside soldiers who sang as they marched past. A black-and-white copy of Hitler's portrait faced us at the front of the kindergarten classroom where we worked the alphabet with a stylus on black slate. To the very young, uneventful days and nights erase whatever adults whisper about war.

I got scarlet fever in Mutti Weil's house and my mother was struck down with diphtheria. Scarlet fever made my skin come off by the handful. I became my own fast-food dispenser. The nuns burned all my things. Whatever was brought to me in the convent's isolation ward was contaminated and subsequently destroyed. A boy in the bed next to mine disappeared after a nun found us comparing our gender identifiers. We gawped at our differences. Years passed before I understood that he was circumcised and what it meant at that time and place.

My diphtheria-ridden mother disappeared completely. Hospitalized, in recovery and then quarantined for months. Eventually, I was allowed to stand on the pavement outside the building to see her indistinct form wave from behind a closed window on the top floor. Whether to guard against the effects of her highly contagious disease or nullify any lingering threats from my scarlet fever remains a mystery, but I was subjected to a form of hydrotherapy invented and made infamous in Silesia. The treatment consisted of a hot bath followed immediately with a plunge into ice-cold water. Daily. After the first experience, neither Ludmilla nor Mutti Weil could make me show up of my own free will. There were days when groups of soldiers quartered in the village were asked to comb the neighborhood to find me, and with apologies and advice about being brave, carry me yowling to my fate.

The sole reliable news service, National Socialist-controlled radio being totally corrupt, was the BBC. "London Calling" had no more ardent fan than my mother. But monitoring the broadcasts had to be done with utmost secrecy. Severe penalties awaited those who were caught, including imprisonment and execution. The radio was packed with layers of pillows before she would stick her head inside to listen, with the volume turned near-inaudibly low. Mostly, I was chased out of the room during the preparation and listening phase.

When we left Langenbrück ahead of the advancing Soviet army my mother took the luggage that was not going with us and bound it with thick metal wire. I helped. Mutti Weil fussed that it wasn't necessary to use heroic measures and promised to keep everything safe. Inside that large suitcase was some of my stuff and I expressed strong feelings about being made to leave it behind. A small stash of photos was put aside to take along on our journey. Saving photos is what people think of first when taking flight, right after jewelry and cash.

The loss of little things is also remembered in detail forever. My step-mother, Ruth Dietrich, adored the Comedian Harmonists and had collect-ed all their records. In 1934, the group and its music were banned by the National-Socialist government for the usual calumnies: not just too many Jews, but also too much American Negro influence. Of everything that was taken from her by the war, the destruction of those recordings in an air raid came especially hard. Seventy years later she still spoke wistfully of losing them. For my mother it was the loss of a favorite lamp, also destroyed by bombing. Everything was gone including the house, but it was the lamp she talked about for years. The lamp was a 1930s electric *Wunderwerk* that changed colors in some clever way that enchanted her.

And there is the loss of spirit that comes when tranquility and all one's plans fall and wither before the destroyer of worlds. Ruth remembered that the waiter had delivered a luncheon of ravioli and just walked away from her table when the radio announced that Germany was at war. She was seated on the terrace of a hotel in Lindau by the side of Lake Constance. It was an especially fine day. Time stopped, she said. The announcer's words hung in the air. Everything around her was still there but no longer had relevance.

After the war, Russia annexed Upper Silesia and gave it to Poland. Ethnic Germans were driven out, Mutti Weil and Ludmilla, too. Driven out and lost except to memory. The photos came through safely, right up until my stepfather died in Gloucester in 1996, when they were casually destroyed by his second wife. What a Soviet juggernaut, the war, an occu-pation, and a lifetime could not ruin was casually lost by indifferent people in a house on the side of a hill in a small English county town. Documents take on increased significance as we grow old. They are clues to who we are, what happened to us and why. Personal treasure is often abandoned in place of fragments of ephemera that chronicle our past. My mother's decision to take photographs out of Langenbrück, for instance. In lieu of the papers that I wanted, I got the bill for my stepfather's funeral. All else was left to rot or tossed away. Conquered eastern German territories were folded into the Russian empire where they remain today, including my maternal grandparent's East Prussia. The "Good War" liberated only Western

The Lost Patrol. Upper Silesia, circa 1943. The hero in shoes and socks had something to say, a trait he carried through life with mixed success.

Europe. It is going on seventy years since we packed that suitcase in Mutti Weil's house. I still want my stuff back.

Running from the westward-advancing Russians got us back into the heart of Germany in time for the war's final gasps. We moved out of Langenbrück ahead of the Red Army on a train that had a small cast-iron

Langenbrück, 1943. The canteen was emptied and the belt cinched extra tight.

stove in the center of each compartment. When the train stopped, which was often and anywhere, adults ran out to fill their bucket (or tin cup or whatever container lay at hand) with snow that could be melted on the stovetop for drinking water. My mother was afraid that I would jump from the compartment to join the fun outside and be left stranded in the frozen wastes when the train suddenly lurched forward again. Thus, we made our way to relative safety deep in the Harz Mountains, northern Germany's version of Appalachia.

Our destination was Elend (literally, misery) near the village of Sorge (worry). Elend was the last place I remember in Germany as an approximation of home. The life that overcame us was a protracted scramble for survival, a surreal experience of temporary beds in unremembered places, not always indoors. And never-ending hunger. We came to Elend because

Mohicans and Merlins

Nor Mars his sword nor war's quick fire shall burn
The living record of your memory.

— Sonnet 55, lines 7–8

Elend, because it was near his last assignment, Nordhausen, where the old gypsum mines were converted to an underground assembly line, "*Mittelwerk*," for V-1 and V-2 rocket assembly using slave labor. Nordhausen concentration camp is infamous. The detail came through a chance remark by my stepmother shortly before she died, more than four decades after the death of my father.

World War II-era Germans know a thing or two about hiding things. In the genre of keeping-secrets-unto-the-third-plus-and-counting generation, not many years into the new millennium our twenty-something houseguest (the grandson of my mother's godson, as reckoned by kinship groupings) spoke of his great-grandfather's long captivity as a POW of the Russians. "POW? That's not where he was," I answered, astounded that no one in the family had ever told him. "Your great-grandfather was tried and convicted as a war criminal. His death sentence was commuted to twenty years."

His crime was service with an *Einsatzkommando*, one of the mobile death squads roaming Eastern Europe to erase Jewish life. The defense offered at trial was that he shot over the heads of the people his *Kommando* had lined up to execute. The boy was flabbergasted. In 1983, his great-grandmother—the war criminal's widow, Tutta's sister and my mother's best friend—grabbed me hard by the shoulders pleading, "I could not have loved a man who did things like that, could I? Could I?"

There was never an opportunity to ask my father about Nordhausen. He was an engineer and released to pursue his life. No charges. No stain?

The *Wehrmacht* hoped to make the Harz into a fortress, the last redoubt of Hitler's war in Europe. Soldiers were everywhere and our house became a *Waffen-SS* command post. Civilians lived in the basement along with the severely wounded who could not be moved. Troops took the upstairs. Our house was among the largest in the village and belonged to the game warden. It still stands. The village was a designated refuge for orphans, wounded soldiers, and wandering evacuees like us. It was here that a general reached down to lift me up to sit with him on his horse. Here, where our gaggle—girls included—found a sack of stick grenades and passed them around in a circle wondering how to make them work. Here, where we found freshly dug soldiers' graves in the forest, marked with rifle barrels stuck in the ground and helmets on the stocks. American and German.

We played in abandoned trucks and tanks and became smitten with collecting mania. Shiny brass bullets, all sorts of badges, bits of military clothing, prized hats and helmets. I pried loose colored metal turn-indicators from abandoned trucks. I thought a treasure had come my way with the discovery of a wooden box full of *Mutterkreuz* awards. Women who lost a son killed in action got one of these, like a Gold Star lapel button given in the United States to mothers who lost a child to enemy action. My elation was flattened when no one had the least interest in trading anything for them. Seventy years on, they are still not worth much.

Postcards featured U-Boat, Luftwaffe, and Panzer aces. Older boys were mad about these portraits. Studio poses sometimes dressed the war heroes in hats worn at a rakish angle, a cigarette held casually, the smoke curling upward. There could be no élan without a cigarette in the Second World War, whatever side you were with. And everyone could hum "Lili Marleen."

The war's distant percussion rumbled night and day. In quiet periods we were let outside amid volleys of dire warnings. Considering the times and the lethal stuff we found, it is a wonder we were allowed out at all, and that no one in my bunch managed to blow off a limb or lose their life.

Every adult in Elend preached not to pick up things we found in the forest. Don't touch ammunition. Heaps of bullets lay everywhere. Loose, in boxes, in belts, in clips, and tucked inside pouches. We let them cascade through our hands like gold coins. Don't climb on abandoned trucks and jeeps and never go inside a tank, they warned. But we clambered aboard just the same. Never touch abandoned helmets or caps, said sternly with waving finger. We always did, except for the helmets on the graves. These were sacred. Head lice were a common affliction.

We were drilled about staying away from roads when planes were overhead. Aircraft machine-gunned open spaces, especially roads and there were dead horses to prove it. When horses lay newly gunned down in bloodied heaps my mother and other women in the village raced out with buckets and knives to hack at whatever meat they could, as quickly as they could. I had no problem eating horsemeat, and still don't. Fifty years later, the Elend village butcher's wife remembered how I haunted her shop.

On a bright, sunny, late winter day, I stood in a field outside the village as Allied aircraft unloaded whopping streams of silver metal foil in torrents of shimmering ribbons. Arms stretched wide, enchanted, I ran into the thick of it letting the strips rain over me, collecting arms full, shouting with glee. Among adult taboos was the one about never to pick up anything dropped from aircraft. There were warnings about exploding teddy bears, booby-trapped rubber balls, and toys especially designed to kill curious German children. The silver shower on that spring morning shocked me with its novelty and beauty. A lifetime later I learnt that the stuff was an English invention called window, or chaff, that it came in different lengths and widths, and was scattered across a wide horizon ahead of an Allied bombing raid to neutralize German radar bandwidths.

Bomber armadas lumbered over us endlessly as they reached for their city targets. Over time, the constant roar got to me. And because I could not sleep under the din made by a thousand Merlin, Boeing, and Rolls Royce engines, my mother read to me. Thus, I listened to James Fenimore Cooper's clunky prose about Leatherstocking in a German translation. *Deerslayer* to the sound of Armageddon. Night after night. Hours piled on hours of Natty Bumppo and Chingachgook, of redcoats and drums on the Mohawk and savage, painted faces. After the war, when English children played cowboys and Indians my adventures centered on trappers and Mohicans. Love of books stuck with me—for sheer pleasure as well as to relieve times of anxiety and crashing doubt.

And what was the bombers' mission in that golden spring light of 1945 when a heap of silver fell into my arms? To turn over and pulverize further the mountains of rubble that had been made by raids on the previous day and week and month. I dare say that the Germans who were soon to be blown to bits were, like Natty's summary of his Indian companion "not altogether without some ricommend [sic] in the way of good conduct." No matter. We were all being properly punished. You could do anything to Germans at that time. Any German, large or small. Gender neutral. All ages. Anything at all.

In Elend, my mother did duty as a volunteer *Wehrmacht* field nurse. Daily, she tended her patients and let me tag along. "Our boys," she called them. She still called them that when the war was long past. I think of them in that way, too. "Men" in their teens, most of them. Our unfortunates lay heavily bandaged, tucked under blankets. Some spoke, most were silent. I wasn't to pester them, she said. On good days they were taken outside in the garden in the sun.

Her uniform included a Red Cross armband. I wanted one just like it and nagged until she had stitched a small copy. Armbands had become a sensitive topic between us since Langenbrück, when I was made to return a small, child-sized Hitler Youth uniform, complete with mini dagger. I was so abashed about not being allowed to keep the things after enthusiastically accepting, that I sneaked to the house of the boy who gave them to me and left it all on his doorstep, without knocking.

As I started to pull on the Red Cross armband and follow my mother outside through a set of French windows, an American artillery shell whooshed overhead. The shell was so low and so loud it might have been an express train passing at full speed through my hair. I wailed loudly. Nothing my mother said convinced me that the gunner had not made me his personal target when he saw my hand tug at that armband. The round fell in the middle of the village killing a boy of about twelve or fourteen, and his mother. We watched as the dead woman's mother, the boy's grandmother, bolted through the streets, crazed with grief. Now and then she fell, got up and ran again. Directionless. Blinded by sorrow. In her anguish she ricocheted into walls and fences, my mother and other women in hot pursuit.

A knot of people shuffled about watching intersecting contrails where two fighters dueled against the blue late winter sky. One of "ours" and one of "theirs." Theirs won. The adults let out a groan and looked away.

Packs of children roamed the roads and woods, chucked stones into the Bode, the little shallow stream that hardly deserved a name of its own, and hunted the detritus of war. One of our forays ignited panic when someone yelled that an aircraft was coming. We scattered like pigeons. I tried to jump over a ditch and missed.

The fall broke my left arm, giving it the appearance of the letter "S." At the field hospital I was put face-up on a tabletop. As my mother fluttered, the *Wehrmacht* surgeon prepared to reset the broken bone. For the anesthetic he had a small glass bottle of ether. The minute quantity he had available was meant for wounded soldiers, not civilian snivelers like me. My size was his main challenge. He could only guess how much ether to use and not kill me. I watched him pour the strong-smelling liquid into a folded white handkerchief, then put the handkerchief over my nose and mouth. I was not quite under when he pulled straight my broken arm.

Two young soldiers departed to lay communications wire they carried between them on a large wooden spool. Several women, my mother among them, held the men tight pleading with them not to go. But they tore themselves free and we stood and watched them disappear into the forest stringing out the wire behind them, the women in tears.

White flags started to appear from the windows of all the houses in the village in mid April 1945. I liked flags but thought that white was blah, said as much, and was sharply rebuffed when I asked about replacing it with the colorful version I was used to seeing. There was only fitful sleep in our basement bunker that night. Fighting above us rolled along, the adults giving a minute-by-minute sportscast-like account of which side was firing and what kind of a weapon. Children were stashed in the far corner, well away from the cellar entrance.

I had a knack for taking apart and reassembling gas masks. We all had been issued one of the canister kits. "Careful with the glass eyepiece. You'll cut yourself!" There was delight in getting the thing out of its metal case, strapping it over my head, and goggling at the neighbors while making funny noises. Wedged in my memory of those nights in the bunker is the bowel-loosening sense of dread that something enormous was coming our way. I did not grasp in the least bit that I was attached to anything that others wanted to kill. I had no clue it was Americans who were coming or that we were the enemy. We felt the gloom in the way adults spoke to one another, how distracted they had become and by their edgy, palpable anxiety.

My mother sat in the middle of a group of wounded soldiers who gathered themselves into a clump at the foot of the stairs. She had a talent for grand gestures the consequences of which eluded her until it was too late. The night was long and I don't think anyone slept much in an atmosphere that was dank and yellow with cigarette smoke, tension, and foreboding. Our air was mixed with dust shaken loose by explosions outside.

Adults murmured constantly, chain-smoking. At daybreak came the sound of wheels, tank rattles, and running feet in the street above. Tension in the basement rose quickly. We heard the front door upstairs open and footsteps cross the living room to the trap door that led down to us. The clutch of soldiers at the foot of the stairs looked up, my mother right along with them. The American soldier pulled up the trapdoor and came down. Slowly. I saw the barrel of his gun pointing the way, and then his boots. As the rest of him emerged, my mother exploded in hysterics. She tore at the man sitting next to her, wrenched his arm in the air, pointed at his sleeve insignia, and shrieked, "Doktor! Doktor! Doktor!" The American gestured for us to get up and come out. Only the wounded could remain. One after the other, we climbed up the stairs.

The US 1st Infantry Division's regimental diary says that the war ended for us on April 16, 1945. It was early morning when we were winkled out of our basement hospital bunker by the rifleman. The SS command post upstairs still had the last meal, pea soup, bubbling in a large pot on the kitchen stove as we filed past. Like everyone else outside every building in the village, my hands were firmly plastered on top of my head, back against the house wall.

We had lived like moles and now blinked in the light. A German soldier lay dead in the garden. "Don't look!" people said. One of the newly arrived Americans walking past us on the other side of the road stared intently at me, slowed, stopped, and then came directly to where I stood. He told me something. I gawped up at him, clueless. He motioned for me to put down my hands. Not knowing who he was or why he could tell me what to do I glanced at my mother. She looked down, smiled, and nodded.

Fifty-five years later, this is the story I did not tell at Buckingham Palace.

Badges were a thrilling discovery after breakfast one morning, scattered willy-nilly along the village streets by a large body of troops passing through in the night. Decorations were worn in battle and these had been torn off and thrown away. The war was over, they had decided en masse. Time to go home. Silver-edged Iron Crosses, black wound badges, all sorts of ribbons and other personal decorations along with epaulets, cloth badges, and collar devices (*Litzen*). Sheets of paper drifted in all directions, all of it waiting to be scarfed up by us. An older boy was first to spot a Knight's Cross but he had no functioning hands. His fingers looked to have melted into his palms. He repeatedly tried but failed to pick up the medal with what might have been his knuckles. The spaces between the bones were bright red. I snatched up the trophy first but was talked out of it by his offer of multiple alternatives.

On a morning after the Americans occupied the village I pinned on as many of the medals as could be made to fit on my sweater, and cheerily marched out into the street, stone deaf to my mother's shrieks from an upstairs bedroom window. American soldiers looked on with interest. Lo, the discovery of the wonders of US Army field rations, beginning with the offer of a cracker sandwich piled an inch high with butter and jam. So thick, the top wafer broke in two. I traded the badges. All of them.

Americans requisitioned quarters throughout the village. We lost our place in the game warden's house and moved into an upstairs room. This was where my mother rocketed inside, grabbed my arm, and pushed me under the bed before diving in behind me. I was not to make a sound. Almost at once an American followed. It took him a moment to discover our hiding place and we emerged together, my mother wailing and babbling nonstop. The soldier was unimpressed and took hold of her but then a second American entered, said something to his chum, and they left together.

No child had seen anyone who did not look like us, so the first glimpse of a black American caused a huge stir. We were mesmerized. He stood guard gripping not a rifle but the ventilation sleeve of a Browning .30-caliber machine gun. I have no idea why that miniscule detail remains so visible. This was the same weapon I came to use as a door gunner aboard my US Army helicopter seventeen years later, in Vietnam. We clustered around the poor man in a semi-circle, inching our way slowly forwards until we practically looked up his nose. When he made a sudden move we scattered like chickens, only to reassemble in the same social semicircle of curious gawkers to begin inching forwards once more, staring intently.

I think he was amused.

In midsummer, our Americans left. Whispers spread that Soviet troops were coming to take their place. All of Elend had the news and many people packed up immediately, my mother included. There would be no getting away after the Russians sealed their Zone of Occupation. And we had all learnt to avoid the Russians. From then until we arrived in Wales two-plus years later, my memory of events is patchy.

We trudged out of Elend in the direction of the British or American zones of occupation, my mother pushing a wheeled cart that held her suitcase. We got as far as the small town of Braunlage three miles away. British troops blocked entry with barbed wire and armed sentries. For the next few nights we slept in the forest alongside countless other people camped out on the pine needles. My mother took her turn at the barricade to plead with the Tommies to let us pass. Eventually, they did. Our goal was Berlin, a distance of roughly 130 miles. The trek, mostly on foot, lasted from June to September. And there was nothing linear about it.

Much of the way we walked in a sea of people, everyone searching for an approximation of their former life. Ex-soldiers mingled with civilians, the uniforms shorn of all ornamentation except for the silvery, pitted buttons and *Feldmützen* (garrison caps) still sometimes worn with élan. Our boys. Only the unmistakable profile of their caps and cut and color of jackets gave a hint of what they had been. Once, when I was thirsty, a former soldier brought me a drink of water in an open sardine tin. Instead of boots, they wrapped their feet in rags, thick bindings of cloth wound up past the ankles.

There were no posted railroad schedules of arriving or departing trains, destinations, and times. No ticket booths, either. Sometimes we took trains that reversed direction. My mother's railway station tactic was to look for a compartment, speak to the people inside, and push me through the narrow vent at the top of the carriage window. She would then race down the platform to the nearest door screaming and jostling her way through the crowd shouting to be allowed to board because *mein kleiner Junge* (my little child) was already inside and alone. The trains were always more tightly packed than a mosh pit so that we sat on our suitcase in the corridor.

The pursuit of comfort once overrode her commonsense and might have ended very badly for us both. People forced to stand tightly wedged together in the aisle groused that the next carriage had plenty of space and how awful it was that no one was allowed to enter. The car was almost empty, they complained to one another. Quite so. The carriage was reserved for Red Army officers. Now alerted and angry and undeterred by prudence or basic survival instincts, my mother squeezed past the other passengers—who tried to warn her—to the door of the special car and opened it, asking the Russians pointblank to be allowed to sit down. Unceremoniously denied, she dug in. Words flew.

A man got up and pushed her back, both of them now shouting. When she still resisted, he pulled out his pistol and pointed the barrel straight at her chest, inches away. The two of them were nose-to-nose barely inside the offending car, its door open. He held his gun level. I stood behind her. The German civilians in the corridor gawped in silence. In an instant my mother pulled me between herself and the Russian and said something to the effect that if he shot her he should go ahead and shoot me, too. His gun held steady a moment longer and then dropped. We had our lives but not access to the luxury of a seat in a near-empty car. I don't remember caring.

What I remember of the odyssey to Berlin exists in a twirling fog in which time, distance, and direction merge in confusion. We slept in fields and barns, abandoned houses, railway stations. Anywhere. On a drizzly day stuck in a city somewhere we found a lone British soldier handing out single sheets of rectangular corrugated Quonset hut roofing. (Brits call the wartime structure a Nissen hut.) He doled out single sheets only. My mother looked doubtful but accepted his offer. We carried our prize to a heap of masonry that had been a house to make a lean-to of the curved tin against the arch of a stone doorway, the only piece of the building that remained standing. We crept underneath, curled up, and slept.

With winter approaching our world was in perpetual darkness. Short days and no streetlights. Not much visible electric light of any kind anywhere. Bone-deep cold. The air reeked of wet dust. On the Cologne railway station platform *sans* walls and roof, I looked out over a city that existed only as broken shapes for as far as the eye could see in any direction. The single standing structure in front of me was the windowless cathedral. The rest was a lunar ocean bed of mounds, broken walls, crazy shapes, roofless buildings, heaps of stone. There's no one left to tell why I was in Cologne on that platform at that time, or where we were going.

Except that two years later my U-boat sailor uncle, Günther Jahrisch, my stepmother's brother, looked at the same scene in the same place, newly released from a French POW cage. A seabag at his feet, beaten, his country and uniform disgraced, his heart near to despairing, he wondered if there was any sort of life left for him.

In some place or other, I was wrapped in a soldier's grey overcoat and fell asleep, comforted by the funky smell of sweat and nicotine. Our long walk took us past a cemetery where the corpse of a soldier, very young, lay in full field-grey uniform in the open on top of a flat, raised tombstone. The end of his long trench coat flapped in the wind. Rain ran down his cheeks. Wooden Star of David grave markers dotted the countryside but when I asked about them—ever the keen collector of militaria—no one could give a straight answer. I knew about Maltese Cross markers and helmets on rifle stocks. Stars of David were a novelty.

We were turned back at military checkpoints, redirected, or confined in place. Sometimes there was food. When not, we foraged. American checkpoints were hopeful things. US troops and their dependents were under orders not to share food with ethnic Germans, and to destroy their own excess rations rather than give them away. But American soldiers— already noted for spontaneous generosity—could generally be talked into a handout. Children became accomplished beggars.

English soldiers smoked thin Woodbines down to their nicotine-stained fingertips, then stripped and carefully saved the remaining shreds of tobacco to be re-rolled later. Russians moved in hydrophobic packs we avoided. My grandmother told of how Russian soldiers used helmets to scoop up water from the toilet bowl, and how they unscrewed and pocketed every light bulb in the apartment. Russians stopped people on the street to take whatever there was of value; watches were especially prized. Every Berliner knew the chant, "Uhri! Uhri!" (Pidgin German for watches).

Zones of occupation and checkpoints defined our world, by demands to show our "papers" and by our common rootlessness. The road led through a mobile American sanitation team where we were herded along a chute to the long nozzle of an enormous, powder-loaded syringe that was inserted first down the front, and then past the nape down the back to deliver an explosion of lice-killing white powder. I hated it and yammered.

On the outskirts of Berlin, a city my mother loved and knew intimately, there was not a standing building in view. The streets were covered with the debris of what had once been there. No lampposts. No street signs. No landmarks. And no one to ask. She stared with mounting bewilderment and started to shake uncontrollably. Then she sat down on the suitcase, her body bent over, held her head in her hands and howled with grief.

This was "*Stunde null*" for all Germany, historian Ian Buruma wrote. Zero hour. The cities were "corpse-towns," Stephen Spender said.

The disinfectant powder did not last. I was covered with lice by the time we arrived at my grandfather's apartment, where my grandmother combed out each critter over a newspaper, cracking its little hard body one at a time between her thumbnails. Their house survived probably because American and British air force targeteers needed nearby Tempelhof airport after the war. My grandfather also did his part by hanging out the national flag of troops who owned the street at any given moment during the street fighting in the final days of the Third Reich, during the battle of Berlin. Mostly he got it right. A wavering line of machine gun bullets along the façade and into his drawing room window was the consequence when he did not. My father had the damage mended with stucco.

An obsessive need to be safe, a full stomach, to be dry and warm and surrounded by silence entered my subconscious, never to leave. The sound of a nocturne playing in another room, *The Wall Street Journal* and a glass of red wine in the garden, Moxie asking me to play, and Max in the tree house—these demarcate my notion of glorious peace, freedom and harmony. So much flash and bang and being yanked out of bed took root in my nervous system. For years I woke up in screams. Until a night at 36, Willow Avenue in Gloucester, England, when I came awake fighting as usual and Mum Trigg, our landlady entered the room. "Your parents are out for the evening," she said quietly. "But I'm here to look after you." "Oh, alright," I replied lamely, and never had a bad night again.

However, the disorientation and heart-pounding anxiety that comes from being shaken awake, by sudden noise or bright lights, never entirely went away. But I actually got to thinking of myself as quite the experienced war veteran until the night I was on the "Harry Potter" in an Army latrine in Vietnam as a mortar landed nearby, signaling a Viet Cong attack. "No sweat," I said to myself. "You've heard this before. Don't rush. Stay calm." I took out my pack of filter-tipped Winstons and lit up, inhaled deeply, took the cigarette out of my mouth and put it in again backwards. Wasted food rattles me. When the server behind the deli counter at Kroger's grocery store cut off the first couple of slices of ham and casually threw them into the trash before beginning a new order, I could have burst into tears and lunged into the bin after them.

Postwar Berlin defined the essence of dystopia. The years 1945 and 1946 brought chaos and cataclysm at every level of social organization on an immeasurable scale. Men between eighteen and fifty years of age were noticeably absent. There was no currency to spend and nothing to spend it on, besides. Allied Occupation-issued scrip was slow to circulate. Hitler-era money was worthless. I played with boxes of *Reichsmarks*. Elsewhere, manufacturing had ceased. Our survival depended on barter and among the most useful, easily traded commodities was a cigarette, followed by alcohol and food, preferably canned. Don't listen to the organic, buy-local crowd. The world's best food comes in a tin.

My focus was entirely on tobacco and food. Children formed packs that bayed after Allied soldiers, scrounging chocolate and chewing gum, cigarettes, anything. With nothing else to do and hugely motivated, we were tenacious. C-rations of blessed memory. Seriously, deliriously, glorious Spam. There was nowhere to go and nothing else for us to do. We ran beside, around, and in front of soldiers, hyperalert to any movement on his part that could mean something valuable was about to be thrown in our direction. Americans were rich and the most sought-after quarry.

Competition was ruthless, especially from packs of boys who had lost limbs, most often their legs. No girls among them that I remember. The small, skinny amputees maneuvered on flat, low-wheeled, homemade dollies propelled by rag-wrapped arms that were also often just stumps. Thus, they powered themselves at breakneck speed toward the common target. They did not hesitate to ram spindly legs if it meant getting to the prize first. On the rare occasions I scored a whole, factory-made cigarette to bring home as the prize of the day, it would be carefully kept aside and used to trade for food. My mother recycled tobacco. Americans never re-rolled smokes. The size of their discarded cigarette butts, often half-finished, was lore. We were in full jump before the glowing remnant could start its arc of descent from hand to ground.

A whole American cigarette was a major find. My first puff came at that time. We associated cigarettes with luxury. I fell asleep soothed and happy in rooms blue with smoke. And smoked myself, of course, beginning as a teenager. Half a century later I got lung cancer. So very many amputees wandered the streets in Berlin's immediate postwar years. Maimed adults who happened to be artists jury-rigged a living selling copies of their work after teaching themselves to paint using something other than their hands. To their signature they added, "Mit dem Mund gemalt" (painted with the mouth—brush held in the teeth—if all the limbs were gone) or "Mit dem Fuß gemalt" (painted with the foot, when it was the arms that were missing). How fierce is the will to survive.

Exterior house walls were often completely missing, surgically re-moved by bombing to leave living rooms open to the world, like rows of dollhouses. Pictures still hung on the wall, chairs positioned neatly round a table, flowery wallpaper framing a couch waiting for someone to sit. A mounted clock hung by the door. Nothing looked disturbed, except the people were all missing and there was no staircase to climb. The risk that these shell houses could collapse at any moment invoked adult warnings if we came too close or looked with too much interest. Prohibitions against picking things up in Elend had their echo among Berliners who united to stop us from exploring—and looting—these skeleton houses. The stuff was hugely attractive. We were sorely tempted.

My mother tried moving to Göttingen, a small town where life was considerably less tense than in the former capital. There is no timeline for the shift of location or much memory of what we did there. And it wasn't a straight shot. We were in Dortmund for a while, as well as some place on the Rhine near the Drachenfels where I almost careened into eternity from something lethal in raw milk. It was in our post-Berlin life that starvation overtook us with bitter ferocity. The years have not much improved the effects on me, except by bursts of conscious effort or my wife's tsk-tsking. The drive to eat with robotic intensity has stayed, for instance. Inelegant table manners to keep in check. A horror of waste. The old "Dad'll eat it!" has now become "Here, Opa. I'm full."

The Red and the Black

The purpose you undertake is dangerous, the friends
you have named uncertain, the time itself unsorted,
and your whole plot too light for the counterpoise
of so great an opposition.
                    —*Henry IV,* Part I, 2.3.11–14

Reductio ad Hitlerum. Godwin's Law says that in any online discussion there is the almost certain probability that a comparison with Hitler or National Socialism will come up. Make it 100 percent certain when the topic centers on the Second World War.

We had gathered in the upstairs bar of the Army and Navy Club on Pall Mall in London for a late sandwich lunch. Merrill Dorman and Jim Metcalfe were there. US Naval Academy classmates, both Navy captains one a nuclear submarine skipper and the other an aviator who lost his father at the battle of Savo Island. Colonel Kieran O'Kelly, not long retired from the British Army, came. Wives, grown children, old friends. My former NATO shipmate was along, R. E. "Bushey" Shrubb. In the early '80s we served together on the staff of NATO's Supreme Allied Commander, Atlantic. Our immediate boss at the time was a pitiable alcoholic who made our life difficult. Thus, Bushey and I were joined at the hip. Bushey's wife, Jo, a retired RAF flight surgeon wing commander, was also along.

Lawrie Phillips came. Lawrie, Bushey, and I worked together at what is now the Allied Maritime Command in Northwood, at the end of the tube's Watford branch of the Metropolitan Line outside London. The group had come together to launch my book at a reception in Churchill's former underground wartime cabinet rooms earlier that morning. Our host was the Honorable Tim Lewin. His father, the late Admiral of the Fleet Lord Lewin, had been a keen supporter of the project, though he hoped that the actual first three volunteers mentioned on the plaque would forever remain anonymous. Admiral Lord West of Spithead spoke. The book was about the twenty-two US citizens who had volunteered for the Royal Navy in the period 1939 to 1941.

Much has been written about the three squadrons of volunteer American fighter pilots and ground crew that formed the RAF's Eagle Squadrons in the first years of the conflict, when Britain stood alone. Seventeen Americans also served gallantly as commissioned officers in the British infantry. Their story has yet to be told. A plaque in the floor of the Royal Naval College's Painted Hall in Greenwich in 1941 acknowledged the first three US nationals who reported to the Royal Navy as sea-service officers, but kept their identities secret. College officials were fully aware that under US law the men could face prosecution at home, even loss of their US citizenship, by violating the Neutrality Act and serving in foreign arms. The first three in the plaque were left anonymous.

Conversation in the club lounge drifted to motivation.

Why leave the safety of their neutral homeland to put themselves in harm's way? The motivating power of a spirit of adventure was eloquently expressed by one of the Eagle Squadrons' pilots, who might have been speaking for most of his fellow volunteers. The answer to the question was simply, "What the hell." Among the naval officers there were some young adventurers, too. A few—like the brothers in *Beau Geste*—came to forget domestic failure. A couple of the volunteers hoped, vainly, to escape their alcoholism. Some were keen Anglophiles. A minority was motivated by their outrage at National Socialist behavior, as well as by a keen sense of duty to civilization, as they saw it. They came via the Ivy League and from well-to-do families and, in one instance, a titled Danish family.

None of them specified that they had come to stop the "killing of Jews and other races felt to be 'inferior' by Germans and others serving the Nazi state," as Fred Taylor lectured me. For a large percentage of Americans and Europeans of the 1920s and '30s, National Socialists were less objectionable than Bolsheviks.

At the club that day, I raised the specter of a different group of volunteers whose motivation has gone largely unexamined, the *tsunami* of Europeans who volunteered to fight on the German side. A million of them. Perhaps more. The phenomenon has its own name, the Anabasis. Collectively, untold numbers of men and a few women from every country on the European continent took an oath to fight for Christianity and against Communism. Service to Hitler came with the bargain, but it was not the motivation.

There were as many as 14 million men under German arms in the Second World War. What are the odds that most of them never saw a death camp, mowed down innocents, or herded anyone to their execution? The habit of blaming soldiers for the cause they fight for and whether they won or not is pretty old, fairly understandable and, *hélas*, growing apace.

"Shoulder the sky, my lad, and drink your ale."

A veteran of the Danish underground who became a professional soldier after the war told me that taking up German arms was initially considered to be a good military career move in Denmark. Eight thousand of his countrymen fought with courage on the Russian Front. There were more Frenchmen who served in the SS than in the fabled French Resistance. Until the thirteenth hour—that is following the Allied invasion of Europe, when American troops were already in the Paris suburbs. Then, everyone was in the Resistance.

With nothing to lose, remnants of French units engaged the Russians in Berlin with bitter ferocity during the last days of Hitler's Reich. Impact scars of different calibers on the outside of the Pergamon on Museumsinsel (museum island) and throughout the nearby Nikolai Quarter are reminders today of French troops barricaded inside. An entire class at Spain's military academy enlisted. Hundreds of thousands of Russians stepped up. All the Don Cossacks, fiercely anti-Soviet, joined.

It is just not credible that so many people flocked to service crematoria or swap out expended Zyklon B canisters and exterminate men, women, and children of the wrong ethnic or faith background. In short, the roots of the Second World War have only been partially exposed.

Bolshevik military and political successes made Europe and America afraid. Governments dithered about what ought to be done, but ordinary people did not waver. Bloody street battles between National Socialist browns and Communist reds mark Hitler's political rise. Men of the Anabasis did not come to qualify for membership in the *Herrenvolk*. Communism threatened them. Dread of the Soviets festered, now and again lapsing into hysteria that infused the Western world from 1917 to 1991. Perversely, the Left today attaches a grotesque romanticism to Communism. The hammer and sickle gets a pass. Soviet-backed, People's Republican forces in the Spanish Civil War hold the moral high ground still. The fiction of Republican goodness lingers.

A much more realistic summary of the conflict is in Duff Cooper's character Willie Maryngton in his 1951 novel, *Operation Heartbreak*. Willie's civilian alter ego is the "mentally negligible" Bertie Wooster of the P. G. Wodehouse novels featuring Jeeves, the butler. All Willie dreams of, all he ever wanted to do since he was a boy, is fight in a battle. Fate and circumstance deny him his wish in the regular army and he has resigned from his regiment by the time of the Spanish Civil War. Any war is better than none at all and Willie decides to throw in his lot.

"On which side, Willie?" somebody asked him at his London club. "Oh, I don't mind about that," he said. "Well, you see," it is explained to him, "either you have to join up with the Reds, burn down the churches and rape the nuns, or else you have to fight for Hitler and Mussolini and probably take your orders from a German officer." "Is it as bad as that?" he asks. "Worse, old boy. You're committing a legal offence by going there at all. Of course you'd assume a false name, but if you were caught . . . you'd probably be cashiered . . . and, oh golly, what a disgrace for the dear old regiment! It wouldn't look good in the papers, I must say. 'Cavalry Captain caught in convent,' 'British officer in crack regiment wins

Order of Lenin,' 'Captain Maryngton embraced by Hitler.' It would break the poor old Colonel's heart." Willie quickly changes his mind.

In Europe and the United States of the 1930s, it was anti-Communism that provoked the strongest reaction, not newspaper accounts of bullyboy, National Socialist storm troopers beating up Orthodox Jews and smashing Jewish shop windows. Except for Auschwitz, causes to explain the Second World War would by now be wholly obscured. Hitler was nothing new. Tyrants have marched across Europe for most of recorded history. Anti-Semitism raised no eyebrows. France earnestly, enthusiastically collaborated in arresting its Jews for deportation. Gypsies were cursed everywhere, including the England of my boyhood, where Jews inhabited a tier below even Irish Catholics.

Americans had learnt from the World War I experience and wanted no part of the new crisis, least of all to save obscure minorities. The America First Committee successfully lobbied against another intervention in Europe. Future US President Gerald Ford was a member, as was Kennedy in-law and Great Society promoter Sargent Shriver, future Supreme Court Justice Potter Stewart, novelists Gore Vidal and Sinclair Lewis, actress Lillian Gish, and the poet e. e. cummings.

After meeting with Hitler and dining with Göring in 1938, former President Herbert Hoover's chief impression was that the US should copy Germany's policy on "public health and housing for the poor." Hoover, who is best remember for his mishandling of the Great Depression, though his reputation for intelligence and foresight is currently on an upswing, charged early on that Washington's biggest folly in the Second World War came "when Roosevelt put America in to help Russia as Hitler invaded Russia. . . . We should have let those two bastards annihilate themselves." He correctly predicted, "If we go further and join the war and we win, then we have won for Stalin the grip of Communism on Russia and more opportunity for it to extend in the world."

US hotels, clubs, corporations, resorts, the military, and Ivy League universities banned outright or resisted Jewish membership by imposing strict quotas. Harvard did not hire its first salaried Jewish professor (Harry Levin) until 1939, three centuries after its founding. (Mid-eighteenth-century Hebrew instructor Judah Monis was not permitted to join the faculty until he converted to Christianity.)

Harry Wolfson became a tenured professor in 1925, but had to fund his salary from outside sources. Harvard's president, A. Lawrence Lowell wrote, "The anti-Semitic feeling among the students is increasing, and it grows in proportion to the increase in the number of Jews." Harvard had no difficulty hiring eugenics champion Charles B. Davenport, who influenced state laws on forced sterilization and miscegenation "to improve the race . . . and control the propagation of the mentally incompetent." Yale honors graduate and Columbia University lawyer Madison Grant received fan mail from Adolf Hitler, who praised his book, *The Passing of the Great Race* (1916), as "his Bible."

Eugenics, involuntary sterilizations, a hierarchy of races with whites on top were accepted truth everywhere. National Socialists took the existential leap by making a true nightmare of it all. When death-factory gates opened to reveal the unimaginable, the Allies suddenly understood why the war had been fought. Except for that, the reasons for the war would long ago have been erased from popular memory. Auschwitz validated the war against National Socialist Germany, but does not explain all—or even most—of the war's origins.

Communists—including Marxists, however hard they reach for esthetic distance by hiding in economic or literary theory, or whatever they think washes them clean of Stalin—still believe that something valuable is bound to be there in the pile, somewhere. They gain tenure by gulling political naïfs in university classrooms. No one teaches National Socialist theory on the difference between Wagner and Mendelssohn, or why Chagall is just an unacceptable mélange of greens and blues. Revisiting the National Socialist era to dig about for something positive is inconceivable except in some small things. Adolf's shadow lingered in the style of uniform worn by the New Mexico and New Jersey state police, and the corps of military cadets at Texas A&M when I was at Fort Hood in the early 1960s, as well as in the architecture of the era, in the shape of the American eagle on buildings of the period in Washington, DC, and elsewhere. In WPA sculptures like those outside the Department of Justice and the National Archives building and, strangely, in the design of the new World War II memorial on the Mall.

American and British self-righteousness based on the foolish notion that in the place of the Germans they would have risked everything to resist the National Socialist regime is hypocritical nonsense. What protects America is never having been there, yet, and having a Constitution that it has managed to hold onto. Perhaps the remaining issue is the fiction or delusion or half-truth so often insisted on that nobody in Germany knew what was going on. Many people did know. But most people, especially in times of trouble, live their lives pretty much with their heads under their wings, trying to put bread on the table and protecting their own as best they can.

When violence is done by a police state, like the process through which a state lets itself become a police state, resisting it is, was, and will always be something else again. Under such pressures as existed in Germany in the 1920s following the Treaty of Versailles and the collapse of the *Reichsmark*, the US today would surely go to pieces and would grasp at any straw on any terms. And it might well degenerate into personal, racial scapegoating savagery. All that is latent here, anyway. And, alas, in most people.

Much of the darkness at the core of European historical memory through the middle of the twentieth century after the Bolshevik Revolution was the threat to its Christian identity, however threadbare and tenuous that sounds today. Tim Foote remembered, "Years ago I knew a French infantry lieutenant who just after the war went on a retreat to Mount Athos. After a bit he got to know a really old, really Holy man who occupied the cell next. 'My son,' the old man asked, 'where have you come from?' 'I've just come from the war, father.' 'And did you win?' Without getting into the equivocal recent record of French soldiering, he replied, 'I won, father.' Long pause. Then the old man asked, 'Then why didn't you take back Constantinople?'"

Sometimes the only strength left us is the knowledge of why we are taking a beating. Sometimes it becomes imperative to turn the page. Alas, I hid inside the cloak of an English identity, nodding and smiling.

Unmerited guilt is a fraud. Self-abasement became postwar Germany's national pastime. An entire industry of myopic historians and pious moralists exists to block any German effort to be free of guilt, no matter the passing generations or change in centuries. If Germans cannot find the self-confidence to take back the good that is in them and in their long history of accomplishment, they will be hectored into loathing themselves to extinction. Italy gets a free pass. People simply skip the part where Mussolini was Hitler's military ally and soul mate and that Italian troops fought against British and American forces. But Italians did not participate in the persecution or deportation of its Jews on anything like the same scale, and that gets them a citation in the Book of Life.

An alphabet soup of East European countries collaborated in staffing extermination camps. Today, all is forgotten. Muslim Albanians in German uniforms committed atrocities that repulsed even their German masters. Amnesia erased the record. The US State Department supports Albanians while the Serbs who fought Hitler tooth and claw are kept at an aesthetic distance. Poles and Lithuanians massed to watch Jews being herded into boxcars. Christian families in Kaunas picnicked on surrounding hillsides to watch Jews being rounded up in their ghetto and loaded into cattle cars. No death factories in Denmark and Norway. The locals would not tolerate them. National Socialists knew where they could operate with impunity. Eastern Europe jumped at the Final Solution to the Jewish Question.

Amnesia all round. Octogenarian SS guards with Slavic names dodge the US Justice Department's efforts to deport them. Eastern Europe, Poland especially, was virulently anti-Semitic and did not object to Auschwitz or Treblinka. No one likes to remember, but France collaborated in fact and spirit for the entire period of the Occupation. France's police force enthusiastically hunted its Jewish population and handed them over to the Gestapo.

Moral courage was largely absent in the French national character during the years 1939–45. Britain felt it was necessary to bomb a recalcitrant French Navy into scrap iron at Mers-el-Kébir because French admirals wobbled alarmingly as they pondered what side they were on. France bombed the British at Gibraltar and fought the Anglo-American landings in North Africa. None of that got a shake in British schools in my day. The wall that is 1950s English history is simply too high and thick and deep to scale, break through, or burrow under. Since 1914, fueled by a scandalous tabloid media, Britons still hang on to a narrow truth about twentieth-century history. No dwelling on complications here. "When we won the war," they like to say.

My heart is with the RAF's Eagle Squadron volunteers and other Americans who left the safety of their pre-Pearl Harbor homes to join the Royal Navy. Their cause is my cause heart and soul, but had I been of a certain age, I know my fate would have been decided in field grey on some ghastly Russian winter battlefield alongside *unsere Jungs*. People fight for their country, right or wrong. The notion of sitting it out in a neutral place is largely wistful thinking.

And so I spoke over sandwiches and a pint in a comfortable room at the Army and Navy Club overlooking St. James Square, but Lawrie Phillips would have none of it. He delivered himself of a warm panegyric on the conflict being really quite straightforward: goose-stepping automatons serving a tyrant's appetite for conquest caused the war. Then he took himself off. A good-hearted man. Decent. Eccentric. Welsh. Passionate. I hated to lose him as a friend.

Lessons and Looks from a Dystopian World

Experience be a jewel, that I have purchased
at an infinite rate.
—*The Merry Wives of Windsor*, 2.2.208–209

Our wanderings from Elend to Berlin and my postwar affection for Americans made me unfit for certain types of jobs. For instance, in 1959 on my first day as an eighteen-year-old, 12-guage-shotgun–wielding US Army prison chaser in charge of military detainees picking up garbage on the base in Baumholder, Germany, one of the inmates asked, "If any of us ran, would you shoot?" I paused. How on earth could I be expected to shoot real, native-born Americans of about my age when I so much wanted to be an American just like them? In response, I doled out my three shotgun cartridges until it was time to return to the stockade, when I got them back.

Borders, barbed wire, hunger, and dreams of a better life cast long shadows. In 1993, after retiring from the Navy and leaving the Navy Department's Sea Systems Command, I was briefly the temporary, probationary, acting press chief for the Immigration and Naturalization Service. In that capacity, INS sent me on an orientation tour of the southern US border, beginning in Imperial Beach, California. Very late at night in a green-and-white Border Patrol SUV way out in the desert between Tijuana and San Diego, a kind of No Man's Land that separates the US from Mexico, the agent stopped to let us both pee and stretch. Lighting one of the cheap stogies I favored in those days, I was shocked to see people abruptly raise themselves off the ground, hands in the air, mumbling apologies. Discovered by me, they mistakenly thought.

There was little talk. Here was an assortment of all ages, young and old, men and women, all of them painfully polite. People with families to support. People who came to work. My heart went out to them at once. "Let them in!" I wanted to shout. "I know exactly how you feel. D'you know how much I yearned to come to America when I was a boy? I've also been halted at check points, at the lawful disposal of uniformed men with guns."

Psychologically, and emotionally, the INS and I were a lousy fit. Gratefully, a year later I moved to a job in the intelligence community where secrets had many uses, including exchange value as an inter-departmental political commodity. Not a violation of security, understand. More like "My secrets are bigger than yours." The CIA has a really first-class cafeteria and a gift shop sells the logo on t-shirts and mugs. Our awards were presented in the CIA's "Bubble." People answer the phone with "Hello?"

Compared with the INS, the intelligence community was a model of clarity. But to write about the experience, of the clash of personalities when directors changed, the accidental bombing of the Chinese Embassy in Belgrade, or the epic cultural reorder brought by digitization and the rest would mean having to give up this manuscript to the Department of Defense for clearance review. I was a press officer of modest seniority and did not collect bags of secrets, but there was an SCI clearance and an environment in which things large and small truly have no place in public. I was actually proud of that clearance, as Bobbie was of hers. We were the US government.

When Falckensteinstraße, 12, was bombed out in 1944, my Aunt Tulla crawled out of the bunker and moved to No. 29 across the street, her brood of girls, my cousins Hannelore, Bärbel, and Karen in tow behind her. Hannelore, the oldest of the three, was tasked with carrying the family's most important papers. Their father, my Uncle Leo, spent the last weeks and months before the battle of Berlin in the *Wehrmacht* digging anti-tank ditch defenses in the suburbs. At No. 29, Hannelore slept on a narrow cot in the kitchen. After the war their tenement became a silent, unheated, and intensely hungry place of echoes and shadows. Lots of people lived there but rarely made any sign of it. Push the light button and race up to the next empty landing before the timer went off, plunging all in musty darkness. With their olfactory receptors sharpened by starvation to bloodhound-grade, residents could detect anything cooking or brewing anywhere in the building. Neighbors popped out of their apartments in animated chatter about the nature, quantity, origins, and source of the aroma. In this barren environment, the smell from a lowly cup of coffee could set people gossiping five floors up.

Making friends with an American was a social coup that led to food and tobacco and real coffee—enough, maybe, for a family to share. Real coffee-bean coffee, not the dreadful *Muckefuck* (a corruption of the French *mocca faux* and pronounced as written) substitute made of acorns. Pregnancies were common. And so was despair. Tulla told of a young woman who leapt to her death from the roof of the building. When her body hit the concrete courtyard the dress split wide open. She lay face down, stark naked, tattered remnants of material fluttered in the wind.

With postwar Berlin as her object, socio-spatial historian Jennifer V. Evans produced a work of phenomenal shallowness, *Life Among the Ruins*. Her take on postwar Berlin is like a PowerPoint presentation on *The Trojan Women* with bar graphs. She warps agony to fit a sallow, contemporary Gender Politics 101 course on human behavior in a text larded with pseudoscientific cant. What price a professional life suspended on rays of women's lib poster sloganeering?

I was a geezer before I found out why we hungered when the guns fell silent. Henry Morgenthau, Jr., the US Treasury secretary and FDR confidant, had a deal to do with our misery. His obituary describes a man who believed "The Nazis were only surface villains, the real rot was in the German soul." FDR agreed. We were starved because we were evil. It is a small comfort to know that it isn't only Germans who let themselves act on demented ideas.

When a people are dehumanized, anything can be done to them. To reduce the surplus German population, Morgenthau was aggressively indifferent to efforts that could have adequately fed us. His policy accelerated death by natural causes. The issue nowadays suffers from being mired in crypto-Fascist politics (the much discredited David Irving, for example), but the fact is that Morgenthau let vengeance overwhelm his humanity and judgment. He acted on a proposal, and lobbied fiercely for its implementation, that Germany should be broken into autonomous states and have its industry destroyed. But for a pastoral Germany to emerge, the Morgenthau plan needed a less populated country.

Former President Herbert Hoover reckoned that the population would have to be reduced by twenty-five million Germans for the plan to succeed. Ten months after V-E Day, just enough food had been imported into the American Occupied Zone of Germany to orchestrate a managed famine that affected children and the old, especially, by slowly starving them to death or making them so weak that they died of disease. The controlled trickle allowed a thousand calories per day, per person, General Lucius Clay estimated in March 1946.

Offal-eaters like me got their calories any way they could. Only sugar beets dug out of muddy fields in winter were repulsive, especially when ice cold. *Vae victis.* The *Chicago Tribune's* Hal Foust wrote from Berlin on February 20, 1947, "Germans are dying in masses, not so much from starvation alone as from illness aggravated by acute malnutrition." Children were dying at ten times the prewar rate. General Clay, who became a hero to Berliners, complained in April 1946 (when we were foraging among the city's ruins) that the United Nations Relief and Rehabilitation Administration was "specifically forbidden to function for the benefit of any but displaced persons," and then only by making requisitions against starving Germans. US soldiers and their dependents were required to destroy their excess food rather than give it away to Germans.

Elements of Morgenthau's scheme persisted for about a year. When it failed, he and his mob resigned from the government. The litany of FDR-Morgenthau instigated cruelties is not equivalent to the horrors inflicted by National Socialism. Those are in a class alone. But in the world of conqueror and conquered during the years 1939 to 1945, they contribute a forgotten perspective on the mirror of evils. In one of history's droll Mac-Guffin moments, the senior staffer who drafted Morgenthau's plan at the US Department of the Treasury—Harry Dexter White—turned out to be a spy for the Soviets.

My mother daily visited an American installation to join other watchful women on the alert to intercept anything edible headed to the garbage cans. Women lucky enough to get a job inside the kitchen collaborated with those who waited outside. One of the insiders supplied us with containers of fat skimmed off soups and gravies. A savory mélange, no less. That and cornbread and teaspoon measures of peanut butter. I was about as shamelessly omnivorous as anyone can be, including unabashed consumption of fish eyeballs when herring arrived on the plate. Nothing was wasted. Brown sugar sprinkled on bread was the gold standard of treats.

It was in the context of the Morgenthau famine that my mother met John Mellion Berryman, a corporal in the Royal Air Force twelve years her junior. Of particular importance, he was a cook. He was also the kindest, most honest, decent, and hardworking of men. And he had the patience of a Tibetan Sherpa. Except for John's devotion and faithfulness, my mother must have asked herself times-squared why she had come to Britain. John was truly poor, from a family in Glamorgan in South Wales that had always been truly poor. Poor in the soot-encrusted, red-eyed, pasty-faced, outdoor-privy, heat-water-on-the-kitchen-grate, shilling-in-the-meter-for-electric-light sort of Rhondda Valley threadbare poor. But what they so dearly lacked in material wealth they made up for in character and courage and voices raised in song. If the shilling ran out before it was time to go to bed they cheerfully sat in the dark, with no letup in conversation.

John, with two stripes on his sleeve (which he would later sacrifice to

Corporal John M. Berryman,
Royal Air Force. Born Aberdare,
1922. Died Gloucester, 1996.
What great good fortune to have
this man as my stepfather.

feed me), displaced no authority whatever and never would. But he was a
good man, through and through. Defeated by postwar Britain's hard times,
he tossed his war service medals in my direction when they arrived in the
post. I put them in the same shadowbox alongside my Army and Navy pins
and the *Kriegsmarine* decorations Uncle Günther got for his U-Boat service. Demobbing from the RAF also meant the issue of a dark blue civilian
suit with a spiffy trilby hat. Men and women wore hats in those days. I got
the hat and mashed it into a reasonable facsimile of a Stetson.

Formidable obstacles stood in the way of so junior an NCO getting
permission to marry a German national who had been married to a Luftwaffe scientist and National Socialist Party member. Also not in my mother's favor was her age. Family chitchat has it that she reversed the years,
making 1912 (the year of her birth) into 1921 to lighten the gap. British
officialdom is unlikely to have fallen for something so obvious. I think

she got the RAF's *nihil obstat* to become one of Britain's first German war brides on record because there were affidavits from Jews who had survived the entire war in Berlin partly with her help. Tutta said she helped him smuggle food and clothing, news and hope to their hiding places. And on a visit to Berlin, he introduced me to a woman who had been on the receiving end of their mission.

Kurt "Tutta" Hennig and my mother afloat on the North Sea. They collaborated throughout the war to bring news, food, and clothing to Jews hiding in Berlin. Why they never married has never been explained.

Papers that might have documented details were left in the attic of the house at the foot of Robinswood Hill, in Gloucester, after John died. Where he found the means to pay for a charter flight from Germany might have been in that box, too. Commercial flights had not yet resumed. Hard to imagine where such a large treasure could have come from, to hire a private aircraft and pilot, but he kept his word and arranged our travel out of Germany. He did that and much besides. There was one failed attempt when my mother and I came back to our room to a chorus of neighbors scoffing, "We told you so!" But on the second try we boarded a six-seat-er, twin-engine aircraft and headed for England. I sat in the front on my mother's lap next to the pilot, quietly vomiting into brown paper bags over the English Channel.

Meat, butter, eggs, sugar, potatoes. If you can name the food, it wasn't to be found on English grocery shelves. People ingratiated themselves with shopkeepers, especially butchers. Everything came with a ration cou-pon and could be had only in minute quantities, if at all. Entirely for my sake, John scraped dabs of used butter from discarded plates after break-fast at the Innsworth officers' mess where he cooked. Marmalade-stained, festooned with bits of toast and egg yoke and bacon grease, he carefully collected the remnants in a bit of wax paper to bring home. The sentry stopped him leaving the base and searched his bicycle. When the wax pa-per wad came to light John was arrested at once and imprisoned.

In the middle of the night, a military police car came to the house to tell my mother that John had been put in the base's "glass house," in RAF parlance. Next day we went to visit him there. His small space had a thick, opaque glass window high up on the wall. There was no mattress. The bed was made entirely of wood and had an upward incline where a pillow would have been. John spent a couple of weeks there and was busted to leading aircraftman. He never complained and always regarded the inci-dent with amusement. I never stopped being grateful for his sacrifice and gallantry. After being demobbed a second time, he was hired by Rotol, in Cheltenham. I don't think he missed a day of work, not even after break-ing his leg a second time playing soccer on the company team. At first, he bicycled the twenty-mile round trip to Cheltenham. Rain or shine. Then he graduated to a moped on which he kept the plastic "Learner" tag until the bright red had faded to a dim orange. He never learnt to drive a car.

All food rationing in Britain ended on July 4, 1954. The prolonged scarcity was partly rigged for the purpose of getting sympathy from the United States in order cadge extra wheat shipments, squeeze out better loan terms, stoke Marshall Plan assistance, and the like. What a sallow world it was. Everything was scarce, including the boots on my feet. Most especially hard to find was meat. Any sort of meat. A tin of Spam was a gleeful treat. In retirement, I found Spam's source in Austin, Minnesota, where Hormel produces the stuff. Spam is the punch line of many gastronome jokes, but to me the sight of a tin gives sheer, visceral pleasure. What a treat!

The Nah-zee

As for thee, boy, go get thee from my sight.
Thou art an exile, and thou must not stay.

—*Titus Andronicus,* 3.1.289–90

Our flight landed at Croydon Airport in time for the national distribution of bananas. Young children, English and German alike, had never seen a banana. It was a grand, ceremonial occasion on which the allotted fruit was passed around the table. We had put up temporarily at the house of a friend, my stepfather's former RAF colleague. There were two other boys in the house besides me who had also never seen such a wonder. Watching the bananas go round took on a formal aspect. When my turn came I took a mighty bite, skin and all.

The postwar years in England introduced a quixotic struggle of fitting in with a new language and at least rapprochement with a peer culture that had been primed to hate all things German. Our time in John Berryman's Wales was not pocked by the infection that later came to mark my life in England. In Aberaman, it was "Boy-bach! Cum an' 'ave some tea then, alright?" And "'ow are you then, boy-bach?" Little boy, little boy. And that wonderful Welsh-ism, "There's lovely for you!" My clan-by-marriage were miners and boxers and soldiers and they all had fine voices. My stepfather was a tenor.

Along with everyone else on Cobden Street in Aberaman, the household at number 15 was as poor as anything I have ever seen outside of Mekong Delta villages in Vietnam. Wartime Upper Silesia had a rustic charm where life was lived plainly. I was accustomed to outdoor privies. South Wales was poor in a dreary, sooty, and grimly Dickensian way. There are parts of West Virginia that give off the same whiff of slag and need. My step-grandparent's front room, guarded by a china dog in the window, went undisturbed except for funerals and weddings. My weekly bath was in a zinc tub set on the kitchen floor. Hot water delivery was in a kettle heated on an open coal fire.

Men home from the mines washed up cold outside, in a bucket. From the waist up. Jack, my step-grandfather, taught me how to fry bacon strips on the grill of a coal fire that was never let to go out, year-round. We walked together along The Line, a cinder path that skirted the mountain above the last row of houses, to see the view of the towns spread along the valleys. *How Green was My Valley* is the romanticized edition. It was the character of the people that saved them from terminal gloom, or rage-fueled insurrection against their London masters for permitting such impoverishment to exist. Ragged poverty was there long before the Hitler war. Men remembered with pride taking part in the Great General Strike of 1926.

Rhondda, Wales, is a place where singing and poetry are national callings. They sing a cappella with resonant voices, full-bodied from the depths of the pits in which they worked and where so many of them met their fate. When coal rips the body it leaves blue scars; my stepfather showed me. They sing in organized choirs or impromptu in pubs. Someone starts, others pick up, and suddenly a world-class concert is born. They sing at bus stops queued up waiting, and after they have clambered aboard. The valley's power has sustained me in bleak moments all my life. We lived there until despairing of a job, John reluctantly went back into uniform, assigned to the officers' mess at RAF Innsworth outside Gloucester. The RAF taught him how to cook and bake. He was superb at it.

By contrast, England was a stern place where children mounted a perpetual terror campaign. Hiding was not an option. John Berryman could not protect me. Finlay Road Junior School drew kids from a surround-

ing council house "estate" known as White City, which the city owned
and let at subsidized rents to pensioners and the working poor. At Finlay
Road my first name changed to Nah-zee. Fights were relentless. Every
morning, something. "Come 'ere, Nah-zee!" "Think yer such a big'un,
Nah-zee?" "Gotta teach the Nah-zee a lesson." "Get 'im!" Whack. Punch.
Jostle. Kick. Spit. Bleed.

I almost grew used to it, eventually building up enough rage to hit
back even when it was useless to do so. Resistance must have an edge to
it. Weak flailing brings jeers and makes worse the torture. Pushback needs
an unmistakable *kamikaze* intensity. Bully & Co. should have no doubt
that there is a price, even if that means a lot of your blood and snot on their
knuckles. They may rule, but not without penalty to themselves. Make it
ugly.

The morning chorus of shouts had already begun during recess when
someone picked up a handful of gravel and threw. I returned the salvo.
Another kid joined in and then another and in a moment the entire school
on the playground that morning turned into a pebble-throwing mob chanting "NAAH-zee! NAAH-zee! NAAH-zee!" I threw back as fast as I could
until an immense fatigue made my arms unbearably heavy. I stood still and
just watched. I might have smiled. Why do faces break into a cadaverous,
rictus grin at desperate moments? Whistles blown like billy-o announced
the arrival of troops of teachers running from all directions.

In his office, Mr. Langston, the Headmaster, gravely opined, "Eric,
we have a saying. 'Sticks and stones may break my bones.'" Then he con-
vened the school and the staff in the auditorium where I was put on stage
next to him. He talked about me. He explained that I was not responsible
for World War II. As my English became fluent I took on the camouflage
of my surroundings. When I had become one of them they lost interest
because they could not see me.

However the mental process evolves. Five years into the English experience I had firmly established a distance with my new cultural milieu.
On the morning of February 6, 1952, Mr. Langston quietly ducked into

our classroom and whispered to our teacher, Thomas Ross. Quietly, they confided to the class, "Children, I am sorry to tell you that the King has died." All but one of the pupils let out a gasp. The exception was me. "Not my king!" I thought instantly and looked around, curious. My allegiances, whatever they could be at the age if eleven, did not belong to poor Bertie or his clan or his country.

Alienation sometimes went overboard. As a volunteer collecting donations for disabled soldiers on Poppy Day, an immensely important national event in the United Kingdom, something my stepfather said made me blurt, "They didn't fight for me!" That bit of witlessness resonates into my eighth decade. I apologized and still cringe at the memory today. John was astonishingly understanding and patient. I ought to have been decked, but all he did was sigh, look sad, and say something like, "Now, wait a minute!"

On my last report card from Finlay Road Junior School the Head wrote, "Eric has done much to overcome his initial language difficulty." He makes it sound as though I had a lateral lisp.

Relief from patriotic Finlay Roaders came at Upfield Preparatory School for Boys, in Stroud, where I was sent after failing my 11-plus examinations. I failed at the most abject level, a calamity of epic proportions that would not be allowed to stand. The daughter of an army officer and minor gentry in East Prussia (my grandfather was Hans Joachim von Wernen, from Königsberg) and one-time wife of a rocket scientist, my mother was having none of it. Her answer was an obscure country prep school in Stroud.

Like the chartered flight out of Germany in 1947, I have no idea how the fees were paid. Most people will shrink to the level of their narrowing financial and class environment. Not my mother. There would be no resignation of spirit in order to adopt the depressed social assimilation that came with marriage to my ex-coal miner, former RAF corporal-cook stepfather. Her sense of social superiority was unassailable, and to the end she never stepped down from her pedestal.

Early in the twentieth century, Lloyd George used Upfield's old Cots-wold stone building, Stratford Lodge, as a holiday home. The historian Basil Liddell-Hart's ex-wife Jessie (née Stone) lived next door; she never returned the balls we accidentally lobbed into her garden. Later, when I came to visit from America, she treated me to lavish high teas spiced with stories of T. E. Lawrence, General Allenby, and Winston Churchill, all of whom had been her friends. When Lawrence spoke of "Herself," he meant Jesse, she laughed. Basil probably owes his reputation as much to her so-cial adroitness as to his writing abilities, but he ditched her anyway.

Life was different at Upfield. White shirts with a knotted pink-and-silver–striped tie, a grey jacket with the edges trimmed in pink piping, and a pocket crest with the motto *Mens et Manus*, Hand and Mind. At Upfield, the playground was mowed grass, the headmaster an autocrat, and the masters down-at-the-heel. Classrooms with their nineteenth-century mul-lioned windows were very little heated. "Warmth promotes germs," we were told. Energetic application of a swagger stick enforced obedience. In my day, flogging boys was still an English prep school tradition. At Finlay Road we were only caned: "Hold out your hand. Palm up! Stop moving!" Years later, Upfield's headmaster was published in the newspaper because he beat his garden plants to promote better growth. He died of a heart at-tack beating his dog. The article included the old proverb:

> A woman, a dog, and a walnut tree,
> The more you beat them, the better they'll be.

I come to dread school as the grave of my self-respect and my hopes. Ultimately, I felt precisely the same way about my future prospects in Britain.

Prime mover behind the 11-plus was Sir Cyril Burt. The exam was an effective sieve in Britain's caste culture. At age eleven or so, we took a test that permanently nailed down our intellectual potential. There were three possible outcomes. The best result won grammar school and a toe

Upfield Preparatory School for Boys, Stratford Lodge, Stroud. Heat was minimal, the masters down at the heel, and the head a tyrant. The author stands top row, far right. April, 1953

in the door of a university, maybe. A middling score led to a middling school with a future at about what Bob Cratchit could expect for himself. Utter failure banished the miscreant to the "Secondary Modern" system of perpetual assignment among other young groundlings-deemed-losers who were shunted into a minimalist caretaker education for a little while longer. Such souls looked forward to enlistment in the Royal Navy as boy seamen at age fifteen, say, or apprenticeship in one of the trades. School leaving age was fourteen.

The consequences of 11-plus test placement were irrevocable.

This is how Britain got its butchers and plumbers, barrow boys and dustmen. People accepted the social version of Dante's descending rings as being entirely rational and proper, and the reach extends to popular entertainment. The plot of Gilbert and Sullivan's frothy comic operetta *HMS "Pinafore"* is all about rank and class. For Jeeves and Bertie Wooster, comic tension depends on the contrast. J. M. Barrie's admirable Crichton places class as the defining principle of civilization. That is, unless the household finds itself temporarily stranded on a desert island outside the force field of Britain's tiered culture and the butler's superior survival abilities trump His Lordship's helplessness. Listen to the voices in *Upstairs, Downstairs*. All the toffs are above street level. *Downton Abbey* hinges on class separations.

For rapt Americans, it is all like watching the curious customs of an exotic species. England goes to extraordinary lengths to separate, to distinguish and publicly clarify the INs from the OUTs, down to absurdist detail. Just one picayune example: Royal Navy commissioned officer, gold-lace rank patterns sorted out the regulars from the volunteers. All kinds of patterns emerged. Color patches between the lace broadcast the professions, like medicine, engineering, and ordnance, and separated them from sea service officers who inhabit the top rung. No royal close to the throne will ever sport an "R" (for Reserve) inside the loop of an officer's rank lace.

In my youth, from John O'Groats to Land's End, everyone knew their place. People were slotted at birth to be cast as props outside Buckingham Palace or the Tower of London, or red-coated Chelsea Royal Hospital pensioners when they grew old. His Lordship's rental properties had their doors and trim painted in a chosen color that reminded his tenants and all passersby who was owner. From the perspective of a close observer of how poor people live and are exploited, I am channeling James Agee's American experience here, but England's working class existed, and to some significant extent still does—to accrue advantage for and serve a chosen minority. In contrast to America, where people re-invent themselves and the country is vast, reinvention in Britain is improbable and there is nowhere to go.

The human subset fostered by this system constituted not only a different class, but also a separate phenotype. Their faces gave them away. They dressed differently. They spoke a different language. The divide went into excruciating detail. Clothing was distinct and worn differently. Under the cloth cap class-marker of what covered their heads, even a simple haircut signaled caste. Most distinguishing of all was the way they spoke.

The first tone, discordant and revealing as Eliza Doolittle's street screech, at once marked a person as *Shudra*, or less. By sight and sound, the British working class broadcast its status and acknowledged subservience. It accepted without question the limitations of status imposed upon them by established authority. People were molded into the shape required by the social and economic tier they inhabited, and which the 11-plus test result validated. Helen Corke described these *misérables* thus: "Ye shall not be as princes. Ye shall be as dwarfs, driven by the whips of class and economics to labor, dwarfed mentally, emotionally, condemned to the mediocrity of social order into which your kind were born, to the petty routine of factory, office and schoolroom."

The Britain of the 1950s suffocated ambition. The place was narrow, provincial, and intensely claustral. A working-class newborn got mediocrity and disappointment for an inheritance. End to end, Britain was a nation flanked by the telly and the chippy. Contentment was a few quid left over for a Friday night's piss-up at the local and a fortnight at Butlin's Holiday

Leaving for a holiday in
Weston-Super-Mare. 1950.

Camp. Hope for a better life was in marking up the weekly football pools sheet, expecting a big win. John Berryman was a keen weekly player, but never gave the class system a second thought.

Nowadays, the English working class has a chip on its shoulder, especially the young for whom opportunity is more limited than ever. A hapless, sullen, and self-destructive cohort with scant hope of a future is still the way of things. Adults continue to "muddle along." Upper classes continue to mimic royalty—exaggerated hats for women, ascots for men—and look to the crown for their reward. The received image of England is enchanting. But it is an idea only. There is no British *zeitgeist* in pursuit of happiness. In England, you make do, muddle through, push on, cope. English dreams are about leaving for a place on the Costa del Sol to mingle with fellow expats huddled together for cultural safety. It's a weekend in Brittany with a bottle of French plonk. England is too small, too densely housed, too socially tiered, too spiritually enervated, and, since the ascendancy of regional tribalism, too ethnically fragmented.

How astonishing it was for me to watch American films that showed a world in which people spoke to one another in English on equal terms, even waiters in restaurants or a private speaking with his company commander. Socioeconomic grouping and education, not birthright, defines people in the United States. And Americans feel pretty confident that they too could be rich or pin bars on their collar with a military commission if they put their mind to it.

Sir Cyril Burt was Britain's equivalent of Hitler's *Reichsleiter* Dr. Alfred Rosenberg, with the edges softened. Instead of literally extinguishing the lives of people who were unqualified to live because of their faith or ethnicity as scientifically justified by Rosenberg's *Ahnenforschung*, Burt shot his *Untermenschen* in the head with another kind of scientific flummery, this one was loaded with a standardized test. It got him a knighthood. The 11-plus exam perpetuated and ratified the English class system by sorting out the dolts early. Individual aspirations were fenced at eleven years, no exceptions.

Some parents could send their offspring to public (meaning, private) schools, never mind the fees. Poor marks had no appreciable impact in public schools. The young Winston Churchill was a wretched student. After Burt's death, it was discovered he had burnt his notes and that his research data may have been fabricated. Rosenberg's end was more satisfying. He was stopped *in medias res* on the gallows.

There is much to love in England. One would have to be insensate not to celebrate the beauty of her countryside or the fundamental decency of her people. It is a civil land at heart. Calm. A "Well played!" for any good effort by home team or visitor. Unostentatious (exceptions are the royals, who get to wear lots of medals). Mistrustful of flags and lapel buttons other than a British Legion lion or a commemorative red poppy on Armistice Day.

At least since 1953, I measure my performance by the values in Nicholas Monsarrat's modern allegory *The Cruel Sea*, as personified in the film. A scene I remember especially involves the moment of comradeship between the captain and Lockhart after *Compass Rose* is sunk, in which Lockhart decides to stay on as the captain's exec rather than accept a new command of his own. Really, they decide to go through the rest of the war together. I tried to remember the lesson during my experience in a NATO command where I was deputy to a deeply alcoholic American skipper. Lockhart, blessed with HMS *Compass Rose's* George Ericson as his captain, did much better.

For a youth with time to marinate in the 1950s, England also imbued a solid, ineradicable sense of humor. Humor is essential in a school where the headmaster explains that warm classrooms are unhealthy, and where his old army swagger stick is applied often and with energy.

Germans laugh. But groups have characteristics and humor seems to me not to be deeply etched in the national character. Germans take themselves quite seriously. Not always, historically, though nowadays there have been signs of improvement among iconoclastic young editors and writers. *Gehorsamkeit* (obedience) comes leagues before *Lächeln* (smiling). Wilhelm Busch, for instance. His popular *Max und Moritz* stories for children chiefly push obedience laced with "Wipe that smile off your face!" His stories end in death by fire, by scalding or frightful mutilation. In *Die fromme Helene*, the emaciated little spinster Holy Helene tipples too much, accidentally knocks over a kerosene lamp and burns to a crisp. But that's not the end. German miscreants also get a metaphysical reckoning. Helene's guardian angel loses her soul to Satan. The story concludes when Busch shows us Helene tucked into a vat of fire everlasting. For tippling. No Beatrix Potter in sight.

German grownups go for irony and satire. The magazine *Simplicissimus*, for instance, or the character Kuttel Daddeldu. Dark stuff that bites. *Der Hauptmann von Köpenick*, a popular amusement is based on the true story of a shoemaker in the old Kaiser's time who put on an officer's uniform and discovered that people immediately became obsequious, saluted smartly and obeyed orders, however preposterous. Encouraged by such mechanical deference, the shoemaker commandeered a troop of clueless grenadiers who followed him to City Hall, which he took over and looted. And there we have an allegory of Hitler's success: put people in a uniform, slap on some shoulder boards, and the German civilian population will knuckle under immediately.

Busch and the Brothers Grimm drive at literature in the same way Father Arnall tells a credulous Stephen Dedalus that sinners are dispatched to hell where they roast for eternity with no hope of redemption. Busch hands German people over to the torturers for nugatory infractions. Günther Grass understood perfectly. The fairy tale black witch in *The Tin Drum* recites that evil is "in you, you, you." Oh, for Puss in Boots and the inanities of a Christmas panto.

It's said that England cornered humor as a defense against the weather. A country that introduced us to the wonderfully smug Dogberry, Mrs. Malaprop's idiom challenges, the wistfully sage Mr. Dick and his kite, Neddie Seagoon—to this day I can hear his voice and start to laugh—Spike Milligan, who knew the moon wasn't made of cheese but some sort of frappe. Out-of-control Basil Fawlty and pop-eyed Mr. Bean. Such as these will rescue the world's sanity. It rescued mine. England's wit and literature saved me from the deepest melancholy. If the best that America had to offer were the Three Stooges and the brothers Marx along with that drippy Jerry Lewis with his spastic gyrations, I would probably never have come over.

I grew up reading "Dandy" comic books and the black-and-white cartoon paper *Film Fun*, in which good guys celebrated their triumph at a table piled with food, usually featuring roast chicken and a mound of mashed potatoes studded with sausages. (Chicken was a rare treat. Between 1947 and the end of wartime rationing in 1954, I remember two roast chicken dinners.) I became a charter subscriber to the full-color, magazine-format weekly *Eagle* comic and hunted Treens alongside Dan Dare, Pilot of the Future.

The country had no more avid fan of Biggles than me. I was at the door of W. H. Smith's for the delivery of each new edition. On the wireless, we had the workingman's master of ceremonies Wilfred Pickles, and Flanagan and Allen making light of poverty with their tender rendition of

"Underneath the Arches." Ears glued to the speaker, I learned to bite my nails listening to the BBC's "Dick Barton, Special Agent." Heroes like Dick Barton were always English, with a supporting cast of United Kingdom representatives: a Welshman (Snowy) and a Scot (Jock). Invariably, the Scot was an engineer.

And there was not only laughter and adventure. For a boy who grew up in the Cotswolds, no poem as affecting as Edward Thomas's "Adlestrop" was ever written. I recognize exactly the moment of magnified silence, the rustle of leaves and songbird chorus Thomas means. I have been there, in Gloucestershire on a summer's day suspended in time. It is a hymn to joy and sure sign of the God of creation.

> Yes, I remember Adlestrop—
> The name, because one afternoon
> Of heat the express-train drew up there
> Unwontedly. It was late June.
>
> The steam hissed. Someone cleared his throat.
> No one left and no one came
> On the bare platform. What I saw
> Was Adlestrop—only the name.
>
> And willows, willow-herb, and grass,
> And meadowsweet, and haycocks dry,
> No whit less still and lonely fair
> Than the high cloudlets in the sky.
>
> And for that minute a blackbird sang
> Close by, and round him, mistier,
> Farther and farther, all the birds
> Of Oxfordshire and Gloucestershire.

Mrs. Berryman's boy, Eric. About 15 years old.

I was a loner in love with flying buttresses and fan vaulting. My secret place was the top of Gloucester cathedral's tower after Mr. Moody, the verger, showed me the hidden door. I scratched my initials in the stonework up there and watched the clouds swirl over my head. I took along the only girlfriend I had in England, Annette Venable, the vicar's daughter, who also put her initials in the stonework. Together over the parapet we saw all the hills and quilts of the shire.

Robinswood Hill, about three miles south of the city center. Up Stroud Road past St. Barnabas Church, where Finlay Road meets the roundabout along Reservoir Road, and turn on any convenient right that doesn't go through someone's garden, straight onto the hill. We hiked to its top countless times. As a scout with the 22nd St. Barnabas troop, I played field games there, learnt tracking skills handed down from the Zulu to Baden-Powell, who gave them to us, measured the height of trees using my stave, defended my side's fort and did any number of extraordinary boy-things.

Mr. Moody and I bonded when I was about ten and he let me toll one of the cathedral's giant bells. His wife worked as a helper at Finlay Road School and had seen the Nah-zee get his pebble fusillade. The lower part of the bell rope was padded to protect the puller's hands, and several feet of rope's end lay coiled on the stone floor. There's a reason for that. "Look, this is how you do it," said Mr. Moody, taking one or two slow, steady pulls letting the slack flow through his hands. "There's nothing to it. Come on, have a go." I heard what he said but missed a critical detail. Down came the rope again and I was surprised at the effort that was needed, the heavy bell making its unseen presence felt way up in the tower and me holding on tight all the while. And that went nicely, but then the unseen bell swung the other way.

I didn't let the slack run through my hands and rose from the cathedral floor as smoothly and effortlessly as if I had been in an elevator. Mr. Moody grabbed my ankles in both of his arms. "Let go! Let go the rope!" he cried in alarm.

From the cathedral top you can see most of the county in any direction and several other counties too, far beyond the Vale and the glint of the Severn River west to the Black Mountains of Wales and the Sugar Lofa. "Loaf," we said. The Severn where we fished for elvers each spring and sold the catch to buyers from the Netherlands who paid well for the delicacy. South and east, the Cotswolds, where hill streams join to form the beginnings of the Thames. West to May Hill where story tells—or we told each other—ninety-nine trees grow, and never a hundredth tree is able to root.

You can see the distant Malverns across an endless cover of hedged fields where Piers Ploughman had his dream vision. Chosen Hill outside Churchdown village and Cooper's Hill where the great cheese rolled annually for hordes of cheering, yelping boys who tumbled along at breakneck pace chasing a wheel of double Gloucester downhill. The Forest of Dean, snug thatched villages of grey stone along narrow lanes, all visible from the top of Gloucester Cathedral. No boy ever had a better tree house.

It was Robinswood Hill we loved most, and I have climbed it often with my parents and my wife and alone and always with a sense of accomplishment and joy. I mapped out my future from the top of the hill and have reviewed life's progress at intervals up there in the decades since. In the last years of his life, my stepfather lived on Stone Cross Road at the foot of the hill, where an immense granite cross of mysterious, unexplained history and antiquity rests flat on its back in a thicket of bushes.

We inhabited an almost vanished world in which tattered pieces of nineteenth-century England could still faintly be made out. The rag-and-bone man's horse clopped its way through the streets, the cart driver shouting a barely articulate "Ragsnbones!" to announce his willingness to buy the eponymous product in which he traded. The Salvation Army Band wandered through town, sometimes striking up unannounced concerts right under our window. Gypsy women came to the door in late summer each year, aprons full of homemade wooden clothespins for sale. Their horse-drawn caravans were elaborately carved and painted. No one trusted them, or their wives or children. They came when the circus pitched its enormous canvas tent down on the Oxlease at the end of Westgate Street, on a field at the edge of the river.

In the village of Painswick, near Gloucester, where I went to hang out with my school chum David Tate, street gaslights were lit each evening and doused at daylight by a man manipulating a long, steel rod. If your bedroom faced the street, for a shilling a week he could be hired to rap an early morning wake-up on your windowpane. Dave and I played in the iron stocks, a reminder of a time when punishment was harsh and painfully public. Shepherds in the hills came into the Royal George taproom in winter evenings to spice their pint of beer by inserting a red-hot poker. Veterans of imperial India, the Boer War, and World War I lived among us to tell of unimaginable adventures.

When November 5 came in sight, I stuffed a human effigy to parade through town with other boys chanting, "Penny for the Guy." We spent money on fireworks for Guy Fawkes night when all the other neighborhood Guys blazed atop a great bonfire, to the accompaniment of sky rockets and cherry bombs in a gaudy display of anti-Catholicism. We roasted potatoes in the ashes; "Murphys" we called them.

But I could not make my life in England.

England in particular and Europe generally had nothing to offer. It had come time to find a place for myself, but I was clueless about specifics except for one defining detail. It was absolutely clear to me that wherever I went it could never be to a country that had the Union Jack in its flag quarter or a crown on its cap badge. Australia was wide open when I began to plot my exit. Free passage and a job at the other end. Canada, too. Not an option.

It was America I wanted. Always had been. When I had the luck to meet an American I always asked where he was from, listened carefully to the answer and smiled knowingly when I recognized the name. It was a notional identification, only. Arkansas, Idaho, Kentucky they'd answer, and we smiled because we could all link the names with Hollywood stories, our chief source of information about America. It was the place names that mattered to me, that sounded musical and strange and familiar all at once. Like Walt Whitman, I loved the sounds of American place names. Like him, I thought of America as an epic continent. The limitless horizon was more than a metaphor. You could take deep breaths in America. You could become anything in America.

> Chants of the prairies;
> Chants of the long-running Mississippi,
> and down to the Mexican sea;
> Chants of Ohio, Indiana, Illinois, Iowa, Wisconsin
> and Minnesota;
> Chants going forth from the centre, from Kansas.

My father tried hard to convince me to return home to Germany, but England had somehow made me unfit for Germany. Ten formative years spiced with Neddie Seagoon, that "little ball of fat that could walk under a piano stool" ruined me for Germany. *Gehörsamkeit* was never in my character. Admiral Arleigh Burke's award to any of his staff that went directly against his specific orders because changing circumstances had made it the right thing to do at that moment was much more in my DNA.

There is something wonderfully compelling about England that remains deep as marrow. Up in Dutch Flat among the mountains northeast of San Francisco, the tubercular English square-rigger sailor Bill Adams wrote in *Ships and Memories*, "I know a high round hill the side of which is full a hundred acres. In April's month one-half that sunny slope is solid flame of fiery California poppy; the other half is all deep purple Indian paint-brush. You may see the hill from far, morning, noon, and eve—a sort of holy hill, a place for prayer and praise. . . . I'll let you have it for a primrose bunch, picked in a Devon lane! Old memories are sweet."

And so they are. While England had no real use for me, it became the model of behavior for the manner in which I wanted to live the rest of my life. But America it had to be.

Getting from Here to There

Since I saw you last,
There's a change upon you.
—*Anthony and Cleopatra,* 2.6.66–67

I applied for entry to the United States a month after my seventeenth birthday and was quickly included in the German quota for 1957. Seventeen was the youngest permissible age for unaccompanied emigration. During the interview phase of the process, the embassy official in London asked me what I planned to do when I got to America. I told him I wanted to be a military policeman. He took me at my word. MPs manned the gates to US bases I wanted to enter. A truly crazed reason, and I count myself lucky not to have been laughed out of the consular office. True to my word, I joined the US Army's Military Police Corps.

It was late April and I was done laying out my clothes and books and mementos and things a boy thinks he can't do without in America. Everything was packed in two brown faux leather suitcases. My window overlooked Conduit Street where morning traffic had started to move along. The boarded-up fireplace in my room had brightly colored decals brought back from foreign countries and cities, souvenirs of my travels through Europe by bike and on foot. There was a large brass-and-tin antique steam engine in the corner by the door. I had never got it to work. The drawers were filled with collections of military insignia and medals with Victoria's head embossed, spanning the years from young lady to wattles.

The Crimea War medal was there alongside those from the Boer War and World War I. World War I service medals, even the silver ones, were almost valueless. Each sterling silver disc had the recipient's name, number, and regiment engraved along the rim. World War II service medals made of a silvery alloy, like half-crown pieces, had no value at all. Except, that is, the ones that came in the post for my stepfather. Those I never lost. They survive in a shadow box with Uncle Günther's submarine badges and my own Army and Navy pins.

The walls of my old room were decorated with swords and bayonets and military things I collected all through my teens. Years later, my mother gave away a choice Japanese samurai sword to a visiting Dutch boy. After she died, I gathered up the remainder of the sharp, pointy weaponry and traded them all for a collection of pewter tankards. I lost interest in those, too. It was a nice room at 33, Conduit Street, but I left to begin the seminal adventure with no trace of nostalgia or hesitation. An eon of yearning was over. I was off to the United States for the rest of my life. Bags packed. Steamship ticket in hand. US Embassy's permission secure. A "sponsor" waiting at the other end willing to give me a bed and a meal.

My step-grandfather came to our Gloucester house all the way from Aberaman, fifty miles and a world away to take me on the first leg of the journey. My parents asked him to be my escort. I knew nothing of his coming until he arrived. I liked him immensely but couldn't imagine why he was put to the trouble. There had never been a problem when I left for long summer months on my own exploring the Continent in 1956 and 1957, when I was fifteen- and sixteen-years-old (and when I reconnected with my father and met his new family . . . those details, page 113), Now, it seems I could not be let to fend for myself by train to Liverpool to find the ship that would take me across the Atlantic. He was good company, all the same. Dad, to me.

America. I hardly dared say it out loud. The Americans wanted me to come and live with them. Their door stood open. Americans did not care where I was born, they just wanted to know if I could work. Americans thought my accent was "cute." It didn't matter that I was German. I could have been a Trans-Alpine Goth and they still would have said, "Come." In my bones I knew it was impossible to fail in America.

Among the things I carried along were my Boy Scout uniform and a letter of introduction from Scouting headquarters in London. There was a Bible given to me by "Mum" Trigg, our landlady in the first rooms we rented in Gloucester, up on Coney Hill where I sat drinking cups of tea with her, listening to yet another daily episode of Mrs. Dale's Diary. I also took an old Norwegian hunting knife, the handle and sheath made of bone, and my prized collection of English county Scout patches. England, Scotland, and Wales had fifty-two counties at that time, and I had a patch for most of them, including a special issue that read, "I was a Scout in Coronation Year—1953." A suit was there, too, made of heavy cavalry twill. And for formal wear, a blue blazer with the crest of Gloucester Technical College (a school in which I had been enrolled for two years) on the breast pocket.

My mother got as far as the wooden gate by the street. Faded and peeling paint identified us as living in "Raglan House," the words painted on the stone posts between the gate. She was quiet, semicontrolled, in tears. The usual vivacity was absent. So was the crabbiness. John looked serious and doubtful. He wished me luck. There were hugs and then I loaded my suitcase into a taxi for the five-minute ride to Gloucester's Central Station, over by the Great Western Road where trains ran north.

We arrived in Liverpool's cavernous main rail terminal in the city's center and immediately took ourselves to the docks to find the *Zoella Lyke*s. I had found passage in her months earlier through an advertisement in an obscure travel guide while searching for the least expensive way to a port near Houston, where my sponsors lived. Intensely parochial horizons left me unprepared for America's vast expanse, though I'd been warned. Instead of the Statue of Liberty, my first glimpse of America was of the Florida Keys and the Gulf of Mexico. Dad and I patrolled the Liverpool docks in the taxi until we found the ship, black and rusting at pierside, looking small and not at all like anything that could make it past the harbor entrance, never mind all the way across the ocean.

The *Zoella* lay dwarfed in the massive docks, her hull streaked and deckhouse badly in need of a coat of fresh paint. We were a bit nonplussed.

SS *Zoella Lykes,* launched in 1940, like me. I was one of four passengers from Liverpool to Mobile, Alabama. May, 1958.

This was her last voyage, we learned. Her class had been the prototype for the Liberty ship design in World War II and she had participated extensively in the Pacific campaign as a troop carrier and cargo freighter. She was just as old and tired and hard-ridden as she looked. I was expected. A crewman helped with the suitcases and Dad gave him a tip. Then he took off his hat and shook my hand. I gave him a kiss and he turned and returned to the station to catch the next train back to Gloucester to report to Conduit Street that I had been safely delivered. I was one of four passengers bound for Mobile, Alabama, where I landed on May 16, 1958.

To pay for the passage, I had dropped out of Gloucester Technical College to work as a navvy in the flourmills of Priday, Metford & Son, in Gloucester docks. I worked the night shift with Peter, a veteran of the trenches in World War I. The war liberated him from having to knuckle his forehead or tip his cap in the presence of the mill owner, he said. One of the warehousemen, an infantry veteran of the Second World War in Burma, got me to believe that the physiognomy of Japanese eyes meant that their vision crossed and stopped cold at about 400 yards. Beyond that range you were invisible and it was perfectly safe to stand up and move about.

We filled sacks with flour that fell from chutes, one chute for white and the other for rye. I took every overtime job offered and came home dusted in flour. The day crew loaded our sacks (at 240 pounds each) into the holds of ships and onto trucks. Bobbie wrote:

A nimble young man from UK
to America worked his own way,
if it weren't for the flour
he sacked hour after hour
he wouldn't be here today.

All true.

Now, What?

This morning, like the spirit of a youth
That means to be of note, begins betimes.

—*Antony and Cleopatra*, 4.5.35–36

My sponsor was an Italian family, the Provenzanos, who owned a Houston-based construction company. The link came through Jimmy Mullins, a GI from Hope, Arkansas, I had befriended in England. By 1957, he had left the Army to become an undergraduate at the University of Houston. Mrs. Provenzano was his landlady. Her brother signed the immigration forms, but a recession had reduced the construction business to slim pickings. When the Provenzanos could not hire me, I became a soldier.

Anglo-German polarities still competed, but mostly I was full of hope and absolutely certain that my life in the United States, whatever it became, was bound to succeed. Seventeen-year olds are mostly hormones on a collision course, but I was sure. Sixty years ago no less than now, America was the land of unimaginable opportunity. Like a kid with its nose stuck against a display window, I could pick out and have what I wanted. An early, unambiguous impression took root even before I left Europe: Americans don't give a rap about where you were born or the tint of your skin. "We got work. You want in?" is the only stipulation. When Jimmy Mullins told me about a basic US legal right being "life, liberty and the pursuit of happiness," I thought he was pulling my leg. Pursuit of happiness is what Americans are entitled to do? How can that be?

I spoke the language, sort of. Exceptions abounded: What's a "rare" steak? Indeed, what's a steak? I came from a country with a "Chippy" on the corner where fish and chips doused in vinegar was wrapped in a sheet of local newspaper. Where gastronomic forays meant beans on toast, egg and chips, or faggots and peas. Edible steaks never featured in menu choices as I knew them. Eggs "over easy?" Okra? Grits? Was cavalry twill really the best material for a Gulf Coast summer? 3.2 beer. "Dry" counties. Police wearing guns. Big, big guns. Texas girls who called me "Honey" as casually as you please. White water fountains. Blacks-only seating at the movies. I stopped a bus when the driver pulled over to tell me bluntly that for me to sit in the back was definitely not OK. Foley's Department store in downtown Houston blasting air conditioning over the sidewalk out front. My roundabout was an American traffic circle. Trunks were boots and headlights were lamps. The cultural vocabulary lexicon was long and perplexing. Same language but a different and very foreign country it was. And overarching all else, the mind-bending immensity of the land.

My England boundaries could not take it in. The world I knew stretched to Ross-on-Wye fifteen miles to the west. Fifty miles to Aberaman was a logistics and travel challenge comparable to coaxing elephants over the Alps. London, scarcely a hundred miles east, was reached only by interplanetary travel, maybe twice in a lifetime. Our knowledge store was based entirely on the fragments of America we saw in movies like Ford's *She Wore a Yellow Ribbon* and the Bowery Boys. Scarcely comprehensible on several levels, not least differences in language. We were cliché-ridden. Chicago was gangsters. New York, skyscrapers.

The Army would not take me right away. I was seventeen and needed parental consent. The sergeant was not persuaded that I had immigrated with permission and that parental consent to enlist in the military was implied. For the three months before my eighteenth birthday, when permission was no longer required, the Boy Scouts of America hired me for the summer to work at Camp Strake, a scouting facility near Conroe, Texas, in the Big Thicket, a fabulously wild area of alligators, alligator gars, copperhead snakes, and caterpillars that had "fishhook" growths along their spine.

Our St. Barnabas troop in Gloucester used World War II surplus British Army tents, none of them waterproof. We cooked on quirky, unreliable primus stoves. Camp Strake had cabins and a central dining hall where the kitchen served three meals a day. All white boys and staff, except for Black Week when the others came. Segregation confused me utterly. Even in the Army, which was integrated by my time, the races separated themselves in the barracks, the mess hall, and the recreation hall.

Two days after I turned eighteen, I filled out a form admitting that a relative—my father and other relatives in the German military—had wanted to do America harm, raised my right hand, and swore an oath to defend the United States against all enemies, foreign and domestic, and was on to boot camp at Fort Chaffee, Arkansas, where Staff Sergeant Cowan, a black combat veteran of the Korean War, awaited our arrival. We worshipped that man. Except for the kid who suffered an epileptic seizure at drill one morning, I think everyone in A-4 Basic Training Company graduated in the hot summer of 1958.

Seventeen-year-olds displace very little intellectual space or force of personality being, as they are, fully preoccupied with the mysteries of their own physical imperatives and maturation issues. What did I offer my adopted country? I stuffed flour sacks in Gloucester, brought customers their vegetables on a delivery bike. During the annual Boy Scout "Bob-A-Job" week, I never turned down a task. However, in the United States, respectable seventeen-year olds are all still in school. What use in 1950s America of an indecipherable English general certificate of education instead of a high school diploma? Years later, Hofstra University gave me sixty hours of college credit for the two years of work I did in England, between the ages of fifteen and seventeen. I was able to graduate in three semesters and a summer school (September 1964 to January commencement in 1966) as an honors graduate. Judy, my ex, was the genius who worked out that one.

My immigrant's wealth amounted to less than $50. I possessed no driver's license and had zero knowledge of the culture except what came from clichés and the movies.

A very few preeminent truths made themselves obvious even to a gormless teen: the need to eat and sleep someplace, and the golden apple of citizenship downstream somewhere. The easiest route led to the military. I was mentally prepared. England raised me with the notion of "doing yer bit." We had all been raised thus. Enlistment in the US Army became an adventure, not a burden.

The US Navy had a waiting list for recruits who did poorly on the universally applied military entrance test, the Army Alpha. Domestic raging at home about the 11-plus exam invoked panic in me that was cemented by the humiliation of my abysmal failure. IQ tests brought down a lead-lined, asbestos-infused curtain I could not part, then or ever. On the military entrance test I scored in the "trainable" category, meaning I could be reliably left alone to dress myself, wipe my bum, and flush.

The Army didn't care. When the recruiting sergeant showed up with his meal tickets I followed as cheerfully as any kid in Hamelin chased after the Pied Piper. A reckoning of sorts came at Fort Chaffee, where I was the only white troopie clearing ditches, pulling weeds, and mowing grass. "Secondary modern" education had its US-adjunct, it seems. In 1958, the Army was integrated but also, oddly, segregated. Opaquely so, perhaps, but definitely apart. On perpetual KP, I liked "Pots and Pans" best, followed by being "Outside Man" juggling garbage and unclogging sumps.

In 1958, my request was granted to be a military policeman and after some confusion (all mine) about what the word "airborne" meant (I took it as providing security for a military aerodrome), the six khaki-clad years followed apace, framed mostly in mud and C-rations. Six years, because for my first enlistment I was sent almost at once to an infantry division in Germany, a division that had airborne at its center. Airborne drops at dawn over the German countryside and directing convoy traffic through small villages; being able to bark back in German at civilian drivers who were annoyed at being inconvenienced. Long route marches with the barrel of my machine gun cradled in my neck. Night maneuvers driving General Hans Speidel—head of NATO ground troops at the time—Rommel's former chief of staff. The sound his head made as it hit the jeep's windshield when I drove into a ditch, and how gracious he was when I cascaded apologies all over the landscape.

At the end of that first hitch, I was little better prepared to meet America on its own terms and re-enlisted. The second tour was a life-changer on steroids. Going into the US military made me part of a great nation. Going to war in its behalf made me part of American history.

Call yourself an American, and you're an American accepted by all. Amazing, and exactly what a boy conflicted about his identity needed. But it took several additional decades to become recognizable. I was going on seventy years of age when it dawned how radically things had shifted in my head, when I stopped parroting what people expected to hear. When I dared breathe a contrasting, point-of-view. An elderly gent in an upscale Virginia Beach retirement community was introduced as a former World War II bomber pilot.

He had been shot down over Germany, my host solemnly added, and then spent the rest of the war as a POW. The old flyer looked modest. I stared back blankly and heard myself say, "Good thing, too! Exactly where you belonged." He was startled. So was I. Bombsights like his put me in the crosshairs and I would have cheered wildly to see his machine plucked out of the sky trailing smoke and fire. Only I had never said so aloud.

Old torments resist burial. My British passport surfaced when we unpacked household boxes in 2003 following retirement. Pages of Belgian and German border control endorsements dated April 11, 1958, mark the trip to Berlin to say goodbye before leaving for America. The page stamped May 16, 1958, by a US Immigration officer in the Port of Mobile signaled the moment I was admitted as a landed immigrant. And there is an entry that registered the amount of money I had been permitted to take with me out of England: £26 10 shillings. Here, also, was the visa good for thirty days issued by the embassy of the Republic of South Vietnam when the US Army ordered me there for a full year. There was the renewal stamp from the British Embassy in Saigon in 1963 that got me an invitation to the Queen's birthday celebration. I was in a battle that day and couldn't go.

In the summer of 1962, a British passport with a visa that permitted an American soldier to remain in Vietnam for thirty days got my CO's attention, followed by his energetic intervention with the Immigration and Naturalization Service. The same official who had flunked my grasp of American history at the first attempt, Houston's INS office chief Billy Chapman, met me at the entrance of the federal building. "Who's president?" he asked. "Kennedy!" I shot back. "Right." I passed the history test. "Follow me," he instructed. I went with him to a courtroom where the

Photo for military passport, Vietnam-bound. 1962.

judge announced an adjournment, put me in the dock, spoke a few kind words about my new responsibilities and administered the oath. I was an American.

The quasi-diplomatic "official" US passport carried by all soldiers at that time in the Advisory Campaign phase of the Vietnam War was delivered by the sweaty hands of a lieutenant on the tarmac at Travis Air Force Base, California, just prior to our departure for Saigon. Thirty-plus years later, when I was the temporary-probationary-acting INS press chief, I found Chapman again. He stayed in Houston and retired there. We spoke for a long time. Thank you, Billy.

The British passport's photograph shows a teen of indeterminate immaturity, wearing an odd haircut crafted by a barber in Gloucester who had been asked to approximate the James Dean look. Finding the passport provoked an unexpected rush of irritation. Like *madeleines* with Proust, the little hardback booklet embossed with the lion and unicorn in faded gilt lettering flung open long-shut doors.

When the passport surfaced, my first thought was a more nuanced disposal. I would renounce British citizenship formally with a polite letter enclosing the passport along with the original British naturalization certificate to Her Majesty's Embassy in Washington. The catch was a fee in excess of $1,000. Pay handsomely for something I did not want? Cryptic correspondence ensued, but they insisted on the money. It was then that I threw the documents away. At about this time, the Norfolk Sister Cities Association hosted a large contingent of British VIPs including a warship port call and a visit by the British ambassador.

I was one of the Association's directors and host to some of the visitors. When we boarded the British ship I was instantly surrounded by a praetorian guard of Royal Navy officers who registered alarm whenever I showed the least sign of moving a few feet beyond their circle. They'd been briefed on my citizenship-renouncing notoriety, no doubt. "Who is this nutter? Watch 'im!" Only American citizenship was legal for a staff officer in the US intelligence community, but the security clearance apparatus that peered into all aspects of my bank account, investments, and personal life never caught on. They were as confused by the German-British-American thing as I was. Other Anglo-Americans in the agency were made to renounce their British nationality, sharpish. I coasted through to retirement unnoticed.

Dual nationality is a disloyalty to both countries.

It was my parents who had initiated the application, in the months before I emigrated. Only my mother got to be British when she married my stepfather. When the Home Office vetting official came to the house for a face-to-face assessment, I was warned not to tell him anything about leaving England for America. In turn, the official admonished me to preserve the naturalization certificate (made out in my British name) together with the attached "Erik Dietrich" birth certificate, as this showed the connection between my German and English identities. Thus, my British nationality depended on the strength of a metal staple. It was cathartic to tear it up, all of it. In the end, I came to the US as a German on the German quota. I could have entered on my old stateless document, and wish I had. Official, certified, validated, and licensed statelessness came as a surprise.

At about age fifteen, I got it in my head to travel. For money I chopped firewood and delivered groceries at Mr. Johnson's Green Grocers on the Stroud Road, and by the summer of 1956 had saved enough to launch an adventure, including purchase of a handsome black-and-white racing bike. John built a couple of panniers for spare clothing over the rear wheel. It was then that I found out I was stateless. The German Embassy in London would give me a German passport (I asked) but my mother threw a fit over use of the name Dietrich, and German consular officials declined to accept the English name.

In lieu of a national passport, Britain issued a credential with the same purpose, a Certificate of Identity. Unfortunately, by signaling statelessness, inflexible bureaucrats in all other European nations stood in line wanting money for an entry visa. A pricey stamp was necessary for every country I cycled through, including the land of my birth. But the object was travel and I'd cobbled together all the required bits including £25 for two months on the road, staying at youth hostels.

Lunatic optimism cannot be deterred by trifling, inter-border details. With the identity card tucked away, I pedaled to Dover to catch the ferry to Ostend, where I continued through Belgium to a scout jamboree in Bielefeld, Germany, and then up to Berlin as far as the border town of Helmstedt, where the Deutsche Demokratische Republik (communist East Germany) started. The narrow corridor to Berlin was tightly controlled. I stowed the bike, got my Commie visa *gratis* ("The DDR does not charge students," the border guard told me) and hitchhiked into the city to stay with Tutta and his mother.

Visiting my paternal grandparents wasn't allowed when my mother was near, but I was alone now. I knew the address and knocked. A stranger opened the door. Mrs. Dietrich had died, the man told me. But old Mr. Dietrich lived with his son in West Germany, My grandparents had two children: my aunt Caroline and a son, my father. I understood the man at once. Not killed. Alive. My father was alive. I found it hard to breathe. Could I have the address, please? "No," the man said, "I'll take your address and send a telegram." He did.

A day later my father flew to Berlin. We took the train to his home in Wernau am Neckar, near Esslingen, where he was on the faculty of what is now the University of Applied Sciences. He was remarried and I had a brother nine years my junior, Rainer Günther-Karl, an astonishingly beautiful little boy. We bonded on sight and remained close until his death of sepsis, in 2006. He was an insanely generous man who helped steer a fifty-foot houseboat down the Mississippi in the early spring of the millennial year. When I got a speeding ticket in Wisconsin, he assembled the arresting officer along with the police station's desk sergeant and clerical staff and me, the perp, posed at the center in the parking lot for a group snapshot.

With the same nonpassport, same cross-border restrictions, and about the same amount of spending money, a year later I hitchhiked to Paris

Rainer Günther-Karl Dietrich, my brother, dearly loved, nine years junior and ten feet taller, more generous than a maharaja on a toot. About 1994.

where you could sign up for the noon meal at the Sorbonne refectory and take all the bread you could carry. That wonderful film *The Red Balloon* was made at about that time. How astonishing to see my world as it was then, in what we wore, in the lack of street traffic, when trades were still done using a horse and wagon. On to Marseilles (1,500 French francs for a visa, *s'il vous plait*), and turn left along the Cote d'Azur. ("You're welcome to join us here at the nude beach but you can't wear those swim trunks," a man explained.) To Italy ("3 Lire Oro," per visa) to Milan, where the police let me sleep in a holding cell when it was late and I hadn't found the youth hostel, on to Venice for my first plate of spaghetti, shared with three other equally impoverished hikers, then up the Brenner Pass to Vienna. No visa. Austria didn't charge.

Hoping to save money, I tried to cross into Germany without a stamp and got caught. Border guards recorded my attempt with a heavily blackened rubber censure in my Identity Card, "**Zurückgewiesen, Schwarz. Autobahn. 12 August 1957,**" and sent me packing back to the Austrians who let me in again, no questions asked. Exactly a year later I was a boot recruit in A-4 Basic Training Company, US Army, Fort Chaffee, Arkansas. To this day, passport controls and borders and visas and questions by supercilious little control-point apparatchiks make my blood pressure leap.

My British passport became irrelevant long before I boarded the steamship *Zoella Lykes*. I removed the few pages that meant something to me and tossed the rest in the bin. My stateless Certificate d'Identité remains an emblem of triumph and survives in its original binding. Discarding British nationality documents remains a liberating moment. Holding on for so many years had been a disloyalty to the United States. No doubt John and my mother sincerely had my interests at heart when they urged the passport's importance. And in a world of displaced persons and dysfunctional governments the document had immense value, and might have been leveraged for my good, too. But I had been stamped "Secondary Modern" and refused to accept the designation. My choices made the passport irrelevant.

Vietnam: 50 Years After

Therefore, to th' war!
—*All's Well That Ends Well,* 2.3.301

Our 1962 departure from Fort Hood came on a wet, windswept September day. A Military Police Company, the first sent to Vietnam, we scattered to postings throughout the country and with our South Vietnamese opposite, the Quan Cahn. I first went to Soc Trang, an airfield in the middle of the Mekong Delta. At Fort Hood, with rumors of deployment buzzing, the base library set us straight about the switch to Vietnam. The name Indo-China was better known. Saigon was "the Paris of the Orient," the travel book boasted. Just a few years later the whole country knew about Vietnam. Not in 1962. At the predeparture briefing, our officers self-consciously hemmed and hawed about what to expect at the destination. At last, one of them took stage center and said we were going to war. Not everyone in the room would be coming back. His colleagues looked at him askance, but he pressed on. I think we were all grateful for his candor. Subdued but thankful.

Standing unprotected in the bucketing Texas rain, the Army Field Band played for our departure. We gawked at them from inside the bus, and laughed. I was a twenty-two-year-old of trifling rank and corresponding responsibilities. A trained doorstop, like privates in any army anywhere in every age. I was put to work alongside my Vietnamese counterparts, I supposed for the sake of introducing Americans and their military organization and equipment in the hostile environment of a bitter civil war that hadn't officially been designated a war at all. Not yet, anyway. No unit

On the tarmac with the 5th ARVN Airborne Brigade, waiting our turn to board a C-47. Tan Son Nhut. Late Winter, 1963. The drop zone (DZ) was Cù Chi.

patch; no service ribbon.

We provided resources in the spirit of, and with goals similar to, the Military Assistance Advisory Group, following President Kennedy's decision to stiffen the Republic of South Vietnam's anti-Communist resistance. By my time, this help included ferrying combat troops by helicopter directly into battle and evacuating their wounded, and trudging alongside ARVN (Army of the Republic of Vietnam) troops.

I went to Vietnam because it never occurred to me to do anything else. Because I knew we have a duty to obey our country's lawful orders and I had an oath to live up to. That I loathe Communism was incidental. But I never went anyplace more reluctantly. My marriage to Judy was scarcely two months old, thus orders for an involuntary and totally unanticipated departure provoked something close to disintegration of the spirit as our time together vanished by degrees under the pressure of a force I could not slow, never mind stop. My feelings about what was happening to my life were in a turmoil for which I have no words, even after fifty years.

The Cuban missile crisis played out during my first few weeks in country. That was when Cuba's dictator invited the Soviets to put in missiles aimed at the United States, and President Kennedy emphatically objected. It was about as close to nuclear war as anything in my experience—or anyone else's—during the Cold War. It was a hugely worrying distraction, but I reckoned I had experience. I'd seen Germany pull itself out of the ruins, and if destruction visited America, I would help clean up.

A dense group of people was pressed together when Sergeant Cau and I arrived in Saigon. We came in from the 5th Airborne Brigade at Tan Son Nhut, the district that also had Saigon's airport, to shop for cigarettes (mentholated, the way Vietnamese liked them) and perfume for Cau's wife, at the military PX downtown. The crowd's back was toward us and they weren't making much noise. We blended in somewhat, or at least weren't flagrantly obvious, because Cau and I wore the same Vietnamese Army airborne camouflage uniform topped with a spiffy red beret, and our jeep was Vietnamese Army, not US. Most likely none of that would have made any difference one way or another because the moment wasn't about the war. This was about anti-Buddhist prejudice by the Catholic majority government. "Let's see what we have," I said. Cau wasn't keen but followed. People readily gave way.

We arrived at the outer edge of the mass of people at the instant the Buddhist monk, Thích Quảng Đức, sitting cross-legged at what I think I remember was an Esso station, lit his match. Instantly, his entire body was enveloped in a burst of black smoke and flames. With one voice the crowd let out a moan in basso profundo. "Let's go," I whispered. Cau agreed.

Đức's act had nothing to do with anything we did or belonged to. His ghastly protest was against persecution of his faith. At that, it looked as if

Cau and Berryman might become extra fuel for the charred figure in the center of the flames. This was no place to linger. The South Vietnamese rulers we helped support were super talented in making themselves obnoxious, hated. They made it tough for us to believe they were worth fighting for.

Over time, I came to know Buddhist *bonzen* a little bit better. Like their Western brother monks, *bonzen* live a quiet, inoffensive life centered on ritual and prayer. Unlike their Western brothers, they are vegetarian. I met a group of them—heads shaved and dressed in saffron-colored robes—inside one of their temples in search of my Rudyard Kipling moment. There was no one to be seen when I stepped through the open door. In a large, tiled-floor space lined with open windows, small metal figures sat in niches along the wall. The main feature was at the far end of the room. Seated on a base that came level with my chest sat a huge statue of the Buddha. A jewel the size of a pigeon's egg was in its forehead.

I sat down on the floor about fifty feet away and looked at this thing. Especially that stone. I could take out my government-issue Ka-Bar knife, jump on the figure's ample stomach and in a jiffy pry that stone loose and have it in my pocket. A submachine gun could deal with anyone who interfered.

Sitting there contemplating loot and mayhem, the sound of quiet shuffling intruded. I turned around to see maybe twenty *bonzen* in bright saffron robes arrayed in a semicircle behind me, about thirty feet away. No one spoke. They looked pleasant, curious. We stared at one another and I rose to my feet. They bowed slightly. I returned the bow and walked back outside. Thanks, Rider Haggard and the rest. So much for a misspent youth reading about empire, adventure, exploration, and the allure of "one-eyed yellow" idols and men who would be kings.

At some point between the Fort Hood band's farewell and the death of a saintly monk, I passed the aircrew flight physical for helicopters and was designated as a door gunner on H-21 Shawnee "flying banana" helicop-

Standing in the gun door on an H-21 helicopter.

ters. Brave name. Big vulnerabilities. Introduced not long after World War II, H-21s were designed for cold-weather work and came into their glory during the Korean War. For service in Southeast Asia, all their stuffing had to be ripped out. Anything to lighten wear and tear on the engines was scrapped. Canvas seats. No insulation.

On-board weapons were World War II vintage. We dropped Vietnamese troops right in the thick of combat. A line of H-21s flying really low hopped and jumped huts and hedgerows, over panicked animals, over people near and far shooting back—or just gawping in astonishment. The crew chief sat in the cargo door firing his BAR. The gunner was at the other end of the aircraft with his .30-caliber, belt-fed, air-cooled Browning firing at anything that moved just a few feet below. We hovered inches above the ground long enough to encourage our infantry to leave as quickly as they could, and to provide bursts of covering fire. Hot, spent cartridges flew inside the chopper hitting the troops. Their cue that things had turned serious.

Extreme roller-coaster rides in rickety airframes with mostly hope and the optimism of youth for a shield. Actual physical protection was medieval. The motor pool cut half-inch steel plates the pilots balanced in their laps to cover the chest area, groin to neck. Aircrew got a flak jacket that I wore, and a set of flak diapers I declined. *Apocalypse Now* uses Huey helicopters that were faster and more maneuverable than our clumsy giants, but the sights and sounds are spot-on. The movie gets it exactly right. Hueys soon replaced H-21s. We didn't think of mounting loudspeakers shrieking "Ride of the Valkyries," and our CO was no Robert Duvall with a love of "napalm in the morning," but the scene captures every bit of the energy, the noise, Mr. Toad's Wild Ride, and the blood lust that came over us sitting in an open door behind an automatic weapon. We practiced our aim on ten-gallon steel drums painted white and set adrift in the South China Sea.

Outside Soc Trang was a leper colony and orphanage, both run by a Catholic religious order. The lepers crowded around, talking excitedly and stretched out stumps that had been hands and arms for me to shake. I was shown where babies were tended. Tiny, emaciated things, too weak to cry above a thin, reedy wail. Or stare, hardly blinking, in pathetically small cots. Malnourished, yellowed, hungry, abandoned, and within a whisper of death. Kept alive by the small clutch of French and Vietnamese nuns. I promptly invited everyone to Thanksgiving dinner. When the day came, our CO had forgotten that he'd given his permission. There they were in the distance, a long line of children separated at intervals by a nun, habit blowing in the breeze. "OK, sir. I'll go tell them it's off."

The CO looked stricken, "NO! Bring 'em in." This was an American base. There was food enough to feed every soldier and the children, several times over. One very small visitor unnerved the troops: the child, really no more than a baby, would not stop eating. Our physician took over responsibility for the leper colony and orphanage. We regularly brought them sacks of sugar, powdered milk, powdered eggs, and anything else we had plenty of. Like my postwar experience in Occupied Germany, Americans had food to spare and wouldn't hesitate to feed the woebegone.

We brought out ARVN wounded, and put their dead in black plastic body bags, day or night. We pried loose the wounded from the viscous mud in which they had been put and to which hours of neglect had glued them fast. ARVN leadership almost never called for timely medical evacuations. The whole Asian attitude about life struck me as being a virtual polar opposite to the culture from which I came. Vietnamese grieved, but there was no whining. They died quietly, sometimes even with what I took to be an apology for the inconvenience and mess they were causing. We transported food and medicine, raw materials, and gangrenous children. My position was at the front and right of the aircraft, just behind the pilots, with my mounted gun fixed and swiveling in a steel bar, boxes of spare ammunition boxes in a row at my feet.

The weapon was fitted with a thick steel pintle that had in it a spring-loaded ball bearing. I still hear the click of that ball bearing as it snapped in place atop the gun mount across the open door. The worst noise that literally came back in stereophonic sound was inside a magnetic resonance imaging machine before my cancer surgery, in 1998. The volume and reverberation is exactly, and I mean *exactly*, like the sound of my .30-caliber machine gun firing inside the metal boundaries of an H-21 helicopter. I thought I would come unglued and if it wasn't for the sedatives inside me, I would have.

Air currents do odd things in aircraft. A gangrenous child was cradled by its mother at the far rear, near the cargo door, far from me and downwind. Or so you'd think. I smelled the rotting flesh along with the mother's desperate attempts to disguise the odor with applications of cheap perfume. God forbid we should be offended by her dying baby.

A smaller gun hung on a peg just inside the door. It was there for the moments when your aircraft landed near or on top of a Viet Cong in his spider hole where the Browning couldn't swivel downwards enough to do any good. Some gunners wanted their near-to-hand weapon to be the

German Schmeisser, of which the US Army seemed to have an enormous collection in Vietnam at that time, passing them out to anyone with the need. Schmeissers fired too rapidly. I wasn't man enough for the heavy .45 caliber Thompson submachine gun that, in addition to its excessive weight, needed a special tool to reload an empty clip. Vietnamese soldiers loved the thing for its macho value, though the recoil effect on their small frames could be comic (as well as risky to the safety of any onlookers). I liked the 9mm Swedish K, obtained from the same Army stocks of surplus Second World War automatic weapons. An obsession with small arms trivia came with the job.

We took gunfire on every mission, milk runs included. Every mission, every day. The sound of weapons loosed in your direction comes through clearly at ground level as well as at 2,000 feet. When bullets rip through the fuselage the acoustic effect is never confused with engine noise. It didn't take much to bring down a helicopter, ours especially. At the beginning, the locals thought H-21s were impregnable. The rumor did not last long.

Fifty-plus years later I still believe that we abandoned Vietnam. The bad guys took over. Like every soldier who served there when the US had operational control, I can say with conviction and without irony, "We were winning when I left." I take to the grave my contempt for the politically illiterate, feckless American youth who were complicit in our desertion of South Vietnam.

Service with ARVN troops was good in all the important ways. They were loyal and generous and brave and protective of me. At Ap Bac in January 1963, when my aerial career started, Vietnamese soldiery took a drubbing; so did we. Don Braman died at Ap Bac, and for the rest of my tour in Vietnam I got startled looks from former colleagues, "Hey, Ber'man! I thought you got killed!" Armies don't run to sentiment. The troops made do with equipment that was obsolete. They repaired their own boots in a climate that rotted leather in a few short weeks. "Ho Chi Minh" sandals made of automobile tires and popularized in the 1960s were a clever adap-

A VC flag for a cravat and a fancy O.K.
Corral type of gunbelt belie the mood.
To be exhausted and not run a foot.
Spring, 1963.

tation by the Viet Cong, like their clever homemade weapons. Who knew that a mortar could be made out of the front strut of an H-21 helicopter? A kerfuffle erupted when some South Vietnamese political Pooh-Bah had their troops remove all armor-piercing rounds from machine gun belts. Fear of another *coup*, it was rumored. From our rice-paddy perspective, rot was most often found in the privileged class of Vietnamese officers. It was a common topic among Americans of company commander grade and below, where I dwelt.

Medical care and equipment were scarce to nonexistent. Wounded

ARVN soldiers were dressed by wives who followed in the rear. Badly maimed ex-soldiers stood begging on the streets of Saigon. Field rations consisted of rice-filled bandoliers worn across the shoulders, the end tied with a bit of string. For a meal, they poured out enough to cook and eat. If there was time, they caught small fish in the rice paddy to add to boiling water. The first meal I shared was like that. They had cooked up the rice and finny bits and put a large glop of the stuff in my cup. After an age, and feeling like an accomplished cultural anthropologist *National Geographic* could be proud of, with a great sense of relief I finished every scrap. At that moment, my smiling colleague reached over to ladle another, equally daunting portion in the cup. My heart sank to my boots.

Vietnamese soldiers' stoic endurance was something to aspire to. Less so, the cultural habit of stopping in the afternoon for a couple of hours to cook and maybe take a nap. Both sides seemed to do this.

Second Lieutenant Bic, a Montagnard, chuckled that it was his howitzer that came closest to the presidential palace in Saigon when airborne troops mutinied against the Diem government. He came from one of the tribal regions where people take a close, personal interest in the men they kill. When Bic killed, he cut open the enemy's stomach, dipped in two fingers and put the bile to his lips. He was in his forties when I knew him and had been in the army for decades, starting with the French. It was a remarkable achievement for him to have been commissioned at all. By his ethnicity, indifference to ambition, and iconoclastic sense of humor, his career path stopped at 2/Lt. He was immensely likable.

Vietnamese soldiers did not grouse. There were times—medevacs—when men died in my arms. Quietly, acutely conscious of what was happening our eyes locked together. I knew the instant a soul departed. The effect was like those soundless, invisible earthquakes in New Mexico, when the ground ripples so quickly under foot that you wonder for a moment if it wasn't an illusion, real and ephemeral, all at once.

There was a good-humored nonchalance about ARVN soldiers that made for welcome company. Ngo Van Nhi and I found the PX warehouse together in Saigon. We wanted some smokes. The Navy Chief Petty Officer in charge *gave* us each a *couple* of cartons of cigarettes. No charge. It was usual in Vietnam for men to hold hands, but I instinctively pulled away when Nhi reached for my hand. He was embarrassed. So was I. We stayed friends, and his last letter wandered about the country for a time before finding me. "A month missing you. I couldn't help remembering of our working days. I never forget. . . . I wish you a good luck on your way of duty. And when we see each other again, I shall give you a good narration."

The narration never got told. Nguyên Chánh Sư, Pham Gia Cau, Is Vô Văn Cơ, Bong Ng-Huu. What became of you all? Pham Gia Cau, you dear brave man who fought at Dien Bien Phu and walked south at the partition of the country, who scoured the brigade's supply store to find me a uniform that fit, to whose capabilities I unhesitatingly entrusted my life, you are ever in my prayers.

Judy had stayed on in New York (living as the dependent of a low-grade soldier in Killeen, Texas, would have been a kind of hell on earth). With a job in the garment district and help from her parents, she kept a home for us in Queens. I came home in late summer, 1963 deafened and migrained, the effects of an explosion and of being knocked about inside the helicopter, attached to my safety harness like a puppet. There had been one hundred and twenty missions, two Air Medals, a Purple Heart, and an ARVN pin that the ever-resourceful Cau masterminded for me for my brief but eventful stint serving with him and his boys. I gave that one to my kid brother. The US medals came in the mail months later. By then it was called the Vietnam War. The Vietnam Service medal came when I was in graduate school. There was a single bronze star on the ribbon, to signify the "Advisory Campaign."

I came home too quickly. Decompression time would have been a mercy. Going over took a week aboard propeller-driven aircraft via Hawaii, Wake Island, Manila, and Guam. The return was on a Pan Am passenger jet to Tokyo and Anchorage to San Francisco with a connection to New York City. My boots still had mud on them from Củ Chi when I landed at Idlewild (now Kennedy) Airport. Readjustment had a pace of its own, mostly slow. A radio playing the song, "Where Have All the Flowers Gone?" sent me into a paroxysm of weepy grief. God knows I'm a German with Wagnerian impulses, but not to that extent. When I couldn't sleep, Judy walked the streets with me at night. There were mystery aches and agonies. I had trouble with my legs. Neither of us knew why.

St. Albans Naval Hospital, in Queens, did not know. Judy's cousin, a physician, got it mostly right. "What've you been doing?" he asked. "Fresh back from Vietnam," I answered and added, "I fought." "That would explain it," he replied. We still didn't know what to do but at least we had a clue about cause and effect. Over time, persistent unease leached away. Crippling migraines disappeared twenty years later at the Columbia Hotel in London, after I had walked around Hyde Park in the middle of the night. Hearing got worse. There was no fear of flying, even after a second unplanned drop to earth when a round severed our hydraulic fuel line. Half a century has interposed itself as a sort of protective filter that keeps unpleasantness in check.

I was discharged at Fort Hamilton, Brooklyn, in September 1964, a few months after Lilly's birth, as the Verrazano Narrows Bridge was being constructed. Metaphor, maybe. A glorious future lay ahead. Six years of Army at my gruntling level is the cognitive equivalent of life on a raft drifting between continents. A BA from Hofstra University and graduate assistantships (no tuition and a small stipend; the GI Bill took care of the rest) at the University of New Mexico followed. It could have been the University of Maine, California, or Ohio, but they were no match for the glorious American West. If I had to spend five or six years chasing a doctorate in English literature, I wanted to be passionate about where I lived. And I was.

Nearing the end of my time, it is New Mexico where I want my bones to rest, someplace in the foothills of the Sandia Mountains.

And So, To Graduate School

My dearest coz,
I pray you, school yourself.

—*Macbeth*, IV

News of a man's death freezes the moment. Ernest W. Tedlock died in the fall of 1988, seventy-seven years old. Doors with rusted locks flew wide open when I heard and I saw again some of my graduate school past, clearly and with sharp nostalgia. Ernie and I had an association that matured into cordiality tending to friendship. This was decades before people hugged one another at every opportunity, not that Ernie would have invited hugging. Cordial was as warm as we got. He was a full professor thirty years my senior, the University of New Mexico's resident D. H. Lawrence scholar, and a mentor, and I was his teaching assistant. During the 1968–69 academic year, my job was to grade papers in a course on the twentieth-century novel. The class mixed seniors and graduate students, more than a hundred of them. They read twelve novels and wrote twelve essays each during the fifteen-week semester. I was the only grader.

Hope of claiming a life of my own under this appalling load depended on reading and marking the mountain of paper as quickly and systematically as possible. Relative speed at shrinking the pile also meant the difference between sanity and roaring into the desert tearing out fistfuls of hair. The aim was to finish somewhere on the same day, never mind the hour. Focus was the thing.

It was impossible to read and comment straight through without twitching. I rested, took long walks, stared deeply into the middle distance, smoked cigarettes, and drank coffee to distract myself whenever patience collapsed at yet another sample of tortured prose, windy generalization, or exhausted bromides. It would not do to punish them with acid commentary in the margins of their offerings or come down harshly, however badly provoked I might feel. As the very paradigm of wobbling insecurity and doubt during my first year of graduate studies—and not much improved by the second year—I knew what they were going through.

The students adored Ernie. For the essay on Tolkien I got several illuminated scrolls bound in silk. Tedlock met me later to review progress and problems. Slowly we built up trust and personal comfort levels. He was and remained a private, introverted man.

The dreaded comprehensive examination was scheduled for the autumn of 1969. Two days of scrambling for answers to questions that more or less spanned the range of Western literature, Greek to modern with bits of Japanese Noh dramas or other Oriental whatnottery woven into the bargain. We never knew what to expect. Our peers in Britain specialize early on. A graduate program in the liberal arts in my day was to toss in the air writers, themes, genres, and eras like so much confetti for us to sort into neat piles, like an idiot savant instantly able to count a spilled box of matches. In the fashion of a John Ford Western, the American academy fifty years ago invoked panorama.

The exam was not just any old hurdle. This was the qualifying doctoral exam. It was definitive. An unsatisfactory offering brought a terminal MA along with a push out the door. To be allowed to stay, the doctoral hopeful needed to clear a higher bar. No one ever properly defined what that meant.

In the 1940s and 1950s, Tedlock worked with Lawrence's widow, the former Frieda von Richthofen, cousin of the legendary Red Baron flying ace of World War I. Tedlock went to see her at the house she built for herself in the splendid isolation of the Sangre de Cristo range, where the timberline gives out to scrub-oak on Kiowa Mountain, twenty miles north of Taos at the end of a long dirt road. The whole region in that part of the Rockies came available for settlement to Union Army veterans of the Civil War, the gift of a grateful nation.

The old soldier who homesteaded what became the Lawrence Ranch broke his body and spirit trying unsuccessfully to make the place work as a farm. His youngest daughter was alive in my time and remembered the hardship of the late nineteenth century's pioneering times. What land remained when the homestead opportunity expired became Carson National Forest. Later, Mabel Dodge of the motorcar Dodges bought the property as a hunting lodge. Besotted with Lawrence, she wanted to give him the ranch, but Frieda was jealous and insisted on trading the manuscript of *Sons and Lovers* as full payment. Lawrence and Frieda, together with Dorothy Brett, Georgia O'Keeffe, and others, became the first free spirits with a dream of building a commune in New Mexico.

Tedlock persuaded Frieda to will the estate to the University of New Mexico. As he told it, the University of Texas wanted the property but settled for an archive of Lawrence's manuscripts. It was the sale of the Lawrence papers that allowed UNM to accept and run the ranch. In the role of all things Lawrence, Tedlock chaired the committee that selected two annual summer stipends, the Writers' Fellow and the Graduate Fellow. To prepare for the comprehensive exam, I needed to do some serious cramming and looked for an *oubliette* of my own. I applied for the Graduate Fellowship and got it. Judy stayed behind in Albuquerque, pregnant with Kimberly, sacrificing any hope of even minimalist luxury by living on food stamps. Five-year-old Lillian took her first big, unaccompanied trip across the country to fly pigeons off the roof with Johnny Spain in New York.

My stipend paid $100 per month, a slight sum even for that time, but more than I needed. For transport I took along a metallic blue moped. With a few clothes and a large box of books, chiefly the Penguin series of literary surveys, I moved into the cabin in late May and stayed until early September when the academic year began again. The poet-in-residence that summer was Edward Merton Dorn. He got the brand new chalet at the edge of the forest, overlooking the big meadow where elk came and grazed in the pewter light of early dawn and the long shadows of evening. Dorn and his very young (she was seventeen, he was forty), very pregnant English wife spent a lot of time traveling. He doted on her. The child that came was named Lawrence Edward Dunbar Dorn for the English writer, the father, and the mother's maiden name.

They called the baby Larry. He was just a few days old when his mother laid him on the veranda in the full, Alpine-wattage of a New Mexico Rocky Mountains sun. "I want him to be a Sun Baby," she said blissfully as Judy and I looked down on the squirming, reddening child. The hippy era, then in its ratty apotheosis, introduced novel ideas about how humans should relate to the natural world. Mrs. Dorn was impressionable and Mr. Dorn too much in love to object.

By the late 1960s, the Baby Boomer generation had grown old enough to pick up a few opinions they construed as divine revelation. They sought a liberated body and soul by way of the commune where life was a celebration of *laissez-faire* sexuality, a pharmacy of drugs (booze being part of their parent's world, which they rejected totally), amid an airy-fairy agrarianism where the women seemed to do most of the heavy lifting. This long-haired, bell-bottomed, body-painted counter-culture drove the new order with the righteous certainty of Torquemada stoking an auto-da-fé. The legacy still plays out forty years on.

Taos was dotted with flower children and their alternative life styles famously in communal settlements like New Buffalo and the Hog Farm, not far from my roost at the Lawrence Ranch. They lived on state handouts and cash infusions from parents. The mostly young, white, middle-class groupies came to northern New Mexico for the isolation and the beauty of it. We had absolutely nothing in common, though I envied them their naked dancing girls. After that summer, I completed my doctorate and took a commission in the US Navy. Mine was a different drummer, entirely. Pity, but I never heard of the three Dorns again.

A narrow dirt trail connected the old homestead distantly to Taos Pueblo in the foothills, up past the poet's new place through the forest and on past the ranch to somewhere deep in the mountains. Early one morning a file of Indians on ponies came by, old men wrapped against the chill in colorful Pendleton trade blankets. They wore their turquoise and silver finery. Eagle feathers hung from long braids. I was thunderstruck by the sight of them. A boy of about twelve, equally magnificently dressed, sat behind each man. The Indian at the head of the column stopped and asked me for permission to water the horses.

No one else spoke. The horses drank deeply and snorted and stamped their feet. From the group of men and boys came the faintest tinkling of silver bells on fringed leggings and moccasins. When the horses were finished the riders remounted, the elder thanked me and then led his band onwards up into the piney darkness.

The original cabin, the place that came with my fellowship, was not big enough for Frieda, who built a large place for herself next door. Mine was the old log and mud-wattled homestead cabin built by a Yankee soldier and veteran of the Civil War, with its carved and painted doors and small porch. Georgia O'Keeffe and Dorothy Brett helped make the building habitable year-round, back in the 1920s and afterwards. The hope was to start an art colony in the pristine wilderness, in love with Lawrence and his vision but not necessarily with one another.

My drinking water came from pipes they laid down, and the long ditch they dug yard by yard from where the stream came out of the mountain. A Taos Indian painted his buffalo mural on the smooth stucco of an outside wall. He was a youth when Lawrence hired him and still active in my time, for touch-ups. Inside were a few of Lawrence's belongings, a pearl grey Stetson of the high-domed style worn by Tom Mix in old movies, a sky blue double breasted cowboy shirt with bone buttons, an old suitcase decorated with faded hotel and steamship labels, and an ancient typewriter on a stand. There was a kitchen, one bedroom, and a large living room with a wood-burning fireplace. It was a glorious place in an unrivalled setting.

The most magnificent pine tree in the world stood directly in front of the cabin. Georgia O'Keeffe lay on her back on a picnic table and painted a portrait of its branches against the night sky to the stars beyond the crown. It was also said that she painted the rising phoenix, a favorite Lawrence symbol, on a tin plate nailed high on the big pine's bough, and the small still life scenes of orchids in simple frames that decorated the tiny Alpine chapel where Lawrence's ashes had been securely imbedded in a concrete block. Frieda's grave was just outside the door. They had to use dynamite to blast the hole to bury her in.

Beyond the cabin, past the sweep of meadowland, is an uninterrupted view of the Taos valley to the snow-capped Truchas Peaks beyond. To the right is the jagged dark rift in the desert floor made by the Rio Grande river gorge. Somewhere in the blue of the west is Arizona. It is a breathtaking place of infinite distances centered in the eye of the Universe.

No mystery why Lawrence was so enthralled. How different it was up there from the coal-mining dreariness of Nottinghamshire. The little cluster of lights from Ranchos de Taos below the cabin and the galaxy of lights from the night sky above did not merely shine, they sparkled and refracted in the clarity of the atmosphere. From the top of a fire-watch platform I sat in the dizzy swirl of the Milky Way.

Darkness brings brisk cold at 8,000 feet, even in the middle of summer. Late one night, with a fire crackling in the hearth behind me, I sat at the table at the front window of the cabin, reading Richard Ellmann's anthology, *The Modern Tradition*, when it fell open half way through Lawrence's essay, "The Death of Pan." I think I felt my hair rise as I read,

> Here, on this little ranch under the Rocky Mountains, a big pine tree rises like a guardian spirit in front of the cabin where we live. Long, long ago the Indians blazed it. And the lightning, or the storm, has cut off its crest. Yet its column is always there, alive and changeless, alive and changing. The tree has its own aura of life. And in winter the snow slips off

it, and in June it sprinkles down its little catkin-like pollen tips, and it hisses in the wind, and it makes a silence within a silence. It is a great tree, under which the house is built.

Kimberly, our second daughter, was born in Holy Cross Hospital in Taos in the summer of 1969. She was registered to arrive at St. Joseph's Hospital in Albuquerque, but Judy came up to visit just once too often. We put Kim's bassinet in the shade under that mythic tree when she was fresh from God and her age counted in moments. Her first experience of the world was listening to the wind hiss through the pine needles, watching the play of light looking up through the branches of the tree with its aura of life and hers perfectly mingled.

Gene Frumpkin, the University's poet-in-residence came for the weekend bringing along his girl friend, Kathy. There never was a kinder, more unpretentious man than Gene. No door separated our adjoining rooms and Gene's incessant whispers and giggles became intolerable. I shouted. Gene said he was sorry. Silence. As we fell asleep, Judy announced that the baby was on her way. Not slowly, in the fullness of time, but soon and at any minute. For a brief and panicked moment the four of us thought of delivering the baby right there, near Lawrence's Stetson.

The ranch manager told us he had experience delivering horses and could do the job. Instead, we risked the drive down miles of rain-gutted track in our 1966 Volkswagen bus to the highway, and into Taos to Holy Cross Hospital where nuns took over. Ten minutes later on that Sunday morning Kim was born. St. Joseph's Hospital in Albuquerque sent back our $150. The deposit covered the entire bill at Holy Cross.

Lawrence fans can be a shrill, persistent cult, especially the women. Frieda had her husband's ashes put in concrete to keep them safe from relic hunters. The lunatic faithful got their bits of true literary cross wherever they could. There is a story that the American poet Witter Bynner ate some of Lawrence sprinkled in his soup, on a bet. Dorothy Brett was the only person to show up in London the morning after Lawrence announced his intention to start a literary commune in Taos. He arranged a gathering of friends to sell them on the notion. They liked him well enough, but not each other. Lawrence did not help his case by getting very drunk on the night of the sales pitch and collapsing on the dining room table.

The one-room hut built for Brett still stands. Its size more resembles a commodious outhouse than a human habitat, but there was room in the homestead cabin only for Frieda. Brett was not easily put off. Brett (the name she liked to use) said that when Frieda exited one door, she would enter the other just to be with Lawrence. By 1969, when we met her, Brett had taken to one of those huge hearing horns, the kind seen in comic books and Victorian drawing rooms.

Eventually, Lawrence and Frieda moved on. Ever restless, never finding peace until his death of tuberculosis in Italy. Brett stayed in Taos for the rest of her life, going down the mountain to town to make her living as a painter. She was an outgoing woman and became a local legend. Physically and by power of personality she displaced considerable space. Her station wagon could be heard scattering pebbles and dust, climbing noisily to the ranch where she sat on the porch, talked of Lawrence days, and wept.

One of the many Lawrence worshippers to come tapping on my door later complained that I had no right whatever to be there. My specialty was not Lawrence, and it was not even the modern novel I was interested in but sixteenth-century ballads, with a foray into Elizabethan paleography. They groused to the University that it was insupportable to let such a schlepp occupy the sacred site and shrine. This thoroughly unsuitable person in this place blighted Lawrence's memory, they said. Entirely accepting was Henry Roth, author of *Call it Sleep*, with whom I roamed the forest looking for edible mushrooms that we cooked in the cabin's tiny kitchen. Roth, just like my father, was passionate about wild mushrooms.

Four or five of us trooped into the faculty conference room in Bandelier Hall to take our exams early one autumn morning. One man stepped inside the door, looked around vaguely, grabbed a wastepaper basket, vomited, and left. It was several years before he tried again. I had no problem sitting down, but the questions were incomprehensible. I was like an orangutan contemplating the Rosetta stone. Detached, bemused, mystified. I could not answer any of it, not one question and stood up to leave. Then it occurred to me that there was nothing else on my calendar for the rest of the day, and I sat down again.

The second morning's start was not nearly as bad. I have absolutely no memory of what I wrote except that I was still writing it when the department secretary, Mary Martin, popped her head round the door and cheerily told us, "Go home." The department gave me a University Fellowship and a Dissertation Fellowship.

Eighteen years late, but I had passed my 11-plus.

Ernie lived out on his ranch near Cerrillos on old Route 10 past the ghost towns of Golden and Madrid, along the narrow back road to Santa Fe. With his wife he built the place room by room, casting each adobe brick and sinking fence posts one by one. The land is strewn with petrified wood, huge chunks and limbs of the stuff. Ernie carved footsteps into the sandstone cliffs to make the ridges accessible as scenic lookouts. A fine place but a lonely one—much as fits a description of Ernie. After retirement he became San Marcos Press and printed books.

San Marcos Press published obscure works: prose by David Garnett and poetry by Helen Corke, for instance. Garnett had been a Bloomsbury groupie in his day and remained the stylish literati. In her grief over the death by suicide of her married lover in 1909, Helen wrote a memoir, "The Freshwater Diary," that she allowed Lawrence to use as the basis for his second novel, *The Trespasser*. In 1970, UNM sponsored a Lawrence retrospective at the Taos ranch. An international crowd of Lawrence scholars came to listen and speak, be seen and parade. Among the participants were poet Robert Bly, the brilliant John Lehmann, who had worked with Leonard and Virginia Woolf at Hogarth Press, American Indian novelist Scott Momaday, and English novelist Sean Hignett, the Writer's Fellow the year after Ed Dorn. Corke brought a handful of dried flowers to sprinkle over

Helen Corke and David Garnett, Lawrence Ranch, New Mexico, 1970. "Tell me, Helen, were you and David lovers? I have always been curious."

Lawrence's ashes.

I chauffeured her and Garnett from Albuquerque to Taos. Corke was tiny and stooped. All whispers and old rose petals. Garnett, robust, direct, ruddy-complexioned. Corke was dignity finely carved in ivory, force of intellect, and great beauty of character. They were Victorians, both of them, among the last of their kind in my time. I tried to listen to every word during the long ride north. Garnett was conscious of his literary fame and that most everyone knew his mother, Constance, who had translated virtually all the great Russian writers. Less attractive, Garnett was not shy about acting the voyeur: "Tell me, Helen, were you and David lovers? I have always been curious," he leaned over against her in the back of the car and asked hoarsely. "No," she answered straightaway. "I understand the story persists but we were never more than good friends who shared similar interests." And she said it sweetly.

Up Against the Wall, M***F***: Delusion in Beads and Bell Bottoms

> All the unbaked and doughy
> youth of a nation.
>
> —*All's Well That Ends Well*, 4.5.3–4

What follows is a screed that pivots on my belief that the United States is the world's last, best hope. Nations, like people, strive towards perfection; they don't commit suicide because they've not yet learnt the knack for walking on rays of light. Points of view forcefully stated make for hazardous territory, as in "Achtung! Minen!" But people, like nations, should not be ironbound sure of themselves. That includes my politics or the manner in which the New Age Movement made a home for itself in my subconscious. With that in mind, here's what I hold as true in the middle of my eighth decade.

The late 1960s brought on a political epiphany ignited by a popular American culture that was determined to change the country's values. And, alas, has largely succeeded. Those of us—war babies, mostly (even the immigrant, former enemy kind)—slightly senior to the restive mainstream, risked being sucked under by a social maelstrom that seemed to come from nowhere. All at once the country's well-fed, middle-class youth rampaged against pretty much anything their parents had believed to be true about pretty much everything traditionally important in America.

Marriage, sobriety, patriotism, respect for authority, sexuality, the work ethic, flag and country, and what once was quaintly known as politeness. Under siege or already mostly all gone. Spray-painted and nailed to the wall. The country sluiced down the drains in the 1960s was largely the America that had attracted me to begin with. Not the America of white drinking fountains and sitting in the back of the bus as it was when I arrived in 1958 in Texas, and which baffled me completely. But the ever-striving America prayed for in the line, "And crown thy good with brotherhood."

The tension between good and evil became fodder for sarcasm or outright rejection. The women's movement became nihilistic. Gender equality, same pay, and a fair shot at clambering up the executive ladder are birthrights and worth battling for. My girls can "woman-up" and do anything. It was the rage and bitterness that I hated, especially the anti-male variety I heard in the language of Gloria Steinem, Betty Friedan, and their ilk. Wither Barkis asking Peggotty, "Come, let's be a comfortable couple and take care of each other! How glad we shall be, that we have somebody we are fond of always, to talk to and sit with. Now do, my dear." Too 1800s and irrelevant in the new century? Irredeemably trite?

The mass psychosis that had young Germans burning books in the 1930s morphed into Leftist nation-loathing in 1960s Baby Boomer Americans. The Greatest Generation who put up with the Dust Bowl, the Great Depression, and fought the Second World War came home to give us the most self-indulgent, hedonistic, morally challenged, and intellectually supine set of boys and girls in history. The world turned upside down. "Charles Manson died for your sins," stenciled in blue paint marked the sidewalk leading to the Student Union cafeteria at the University of New Mexico in 1970. Only wittering lunacy can account for such as this.

The liquor cabinet was swapped for drugs. Civility collapsed under the assault of in-your-face confrontation. Power was identified with "The Man" and the man had nothing valid to say. The man—invariably white—devolved to anyone in a responsible job, especially those in a police or military uniform. William Burroughs's *Naked Lunch* tale of drugs, anarchy, and vulgarity became a kind of *Das Kapital, Mein Kampf*, and *The Little Red Book* rolled in one for undergraduates who confused their self-centered bender with enlightened altruism. It was never clear to me why everyone was so belligerent or so unhappy. America never stopped being my pot at rainbow's end. What was the matter with me?

Awakening came in fits and starts, first by way of support for a cause that appealed to my liberal, populist side. I had one then. The other sunrise came about when fellow graduate students in the English department caught anti-Vietnam War fever. Symptoms included thoroughly denouncing the United States. The point was crudely illuminated with the German spelling, Amerika. Get it? National Socialists were in charge. University students organized themselves into draft counseling cells that advised people to leave for Canada or Sweden. My wife joined.

That's when I made application for a commission in the US Navy. Judy's draft counseling advising notwithstanding. We laughed about our contrasting beliefs. In 1968, when I applied for a Navy commission I was confronted with the same IQ test, same failure as before. I wrote to the Secretary of the Navy to explain an obvious—to me—disconnect. I had an honors baccalaureate followed by straight-A masters and doctoral work studded with fellowships. Perhaps a record of ringing academic success merited another look at my candidacy? The Navy agreed. Taking the test was required, however, passing was optional for a direct commission in public affairs or naval intelligence. I picked public affairs, though I later retired from the intelligence community.

It took another sixteen years and Jimmy Carter to turn me from a liberal to a grumpy conservative. I gave up on *The New York Review of Books* and Noam Chomsky at about the same time.

Music is among art's saddest victims. Cole Porter's "So in Love with You am I" has given over to Notorious B.I.G. who entertains with "Girls pee pee when they see me." What happened to Lerner and Loewe's "There's a smile on my face / For the whole human race?" Franz Léhar's merry widow took off all her clothes for *Hair* and lit a joint.

Violence dominated the 1960s, and not only in Vietnam. "Up against the wall!" was shouted and placarded and sprayed on walls. Personal restraint gave way to "If it feels good, do it." Nothing was worth fighting for. "Make love not war" they advertised and remonstrated, with Churchill's old "V for Victory" gesture recast into a peace sign. The Communist clenched-fist salute became *de rigueur*, along with naked couplings in public places. Non-negotiable demands were enforced with the sit-in. Hedonism shot through with preening righteousness scrambled to march, shout, and erect barricades against traditional America.

The Hitler salute remained in poor taste. But that is exactly what this was about. Here were the Brown Shirts of our time, smearing hatred on shop windows, burning books, terrorizing passersby. It was all about turning established culture on its ear, preferably by violent means. "Up against the wall, Motherf...er" was not an idle street cry in its day. Fascism *cum* Bolshevism decked in headband and beads.

Norman Mailer's panegyric on the orgasm helped stoke the sexual liberation that powered the anything-goes '70s. A doctoral student at a prestigious university spoke matter-of-factly and with no small sense of personal pride of her superiority in orgies. Her husband was left far behind in the tally of lovers for which each kept score. Both of them demonstrated against the Shah of Iran and opposed the war in Vietnam. Their social life was peppered with LSD, cocaine, pot. They took endless quantities of money from their parents.

Some of the rest of us went less colorfully to perdition during the sexual revolution. Plain serial adultery did the job, and a descent into licentiousness and the inability to anticipate the range of personal destruction. I got drunk on Gide, Camus, Anouilh, and Becket. Existentialism. The genre suited a crisis of faith as well as memories of Indo-China filtered through the blue haze and acrid smell of Gauloises cigarettes. And Nietzsche. I drowned in the Dionysian and Apollonian dichotomy, choosing the former every time.

When do you know you've had enough until you've had more than enough! A downward spiral is hard to stop short of madness or a bullet. Even *faux* intellectual intensity can kill. The only time I remember saying no is when I dodged my dissertation director's earnest pitch to stay and wait for his lover, Miss Frito-Lay. He wanted so badly for me to be there for the girl's arrival. Her husband drove a delivery truck for the potato chip brand.

The era's forceful, gleeful abandonment of traditional morality trivialized life itself. An iron harpoon landed with such subtlety, decades passed before I realized it was there at all sticking straight out of my chest. For entirely selfish reasons, for my convenience alone, I insisted on aborting my child. As it happened, a son. I was poor. Starting out. Meeting ends. No room here for a new baby. None. Make it go away. Everyone does it. Sometimes now I catch a glimpse when he turns the corner into another room. Sometimes, only the silence that comes immediately after the sound of his voice. I stare at where he was. I tell God. And tell, and tell. The shaft gets thicker as I age. It is harder to see around.

Then, I thought of myself as a laissez-faire Democrat with sympathies for populist causes. Reies Tijerina and his raid on the courthouse in Tierra Amarillo, New Mexico, inspired my liberal moment. Tijerina blended Bible waving with peasant revolt. He took up the cry that land once owned by Mexico but taken by the United States after the Mexican War should be returned. That was the war for which Henry David Thoreau refused to pay his taxes, and the war Ulysses S. Grant declared as "one of the most unjust ever waged by a stronger against a weaker nation."

The peace treaty of Guadalupe Hidalgo guaranteed former citizens of Mexico rights to the land they owned prior to the annexation of what became the New Mexico Territory. The most charitable explanation of what went wrong is that land deeds and equity got muddled in the transition of governments. Former Mexican landowners were pushed aside by the irresistible force of Conestoga wagons and a railroad loaded with people headed west to settle new territory. One hundred and twenty years later, Tijerina stood up to reaffirm old rights and restore property to the descendants of the original owners. He named his movement Alianza Federal de Pueblos Libres. Alianza, for short.

It seemed like a good thing and I became a regular at Alianza headquarters in Albuquerque, a dilapidated building fronting West Central Avenue near the edge of town. Elderly Hispanic women—superb cooks—staffed the kitchen and the smell of fresh posole on the stove was a powerful incentive.

Tijerina had an old-world style and manners to match. He was diffident, shy but welcoming, and a bit wary of volunteer Anglos bearing gifts. He was a handsome man, brave, probably a little mad, but not nearly ruthless enough to be Horatius at the bridge holding off attacking hordes. In the end, and for assorted reasons including mental fragility, his effort did not succeed. My summer job that year was with the New Mexico Department of Human Services, and I offered Tijerina help when people asked questions about their welfare benefits. I had learnt eligibility rules and knew how to complete the application forms.

Mostly, I wrote articles for a movement journal that was published in a bilingual edition by Betty Sutherland, aka Betita Martinez, and Beverly Axelrod. The two women founded a newspaper, *El Grito del Norte*—the Cry of the North—a name inspired by Pancho Villa's army in the Mexican Revolution, the División del Norte. Axelrod was an attorney deep into extreme left causes. So left, that the red of Bolshevism and the brown of National Socialism bled together.

Axelrod's correspondence with Eldridge Cleaver became the basis of the latter's popular, 1968 anti-White rant *Soul on Ice*. The book celebrates rape as a legitimate act of revenge against people of European ancestry. To be white is to be oppressive became an axiom among youth in the United States and Europe. Axelrod's other clients included Dennis Banks, the American Indian Movement zealot, and Youth International Party's Jerry Rubin. The names are obscure footnotes to an era now barely remembered, but in the 1960s and 1970s these men defined the age. A photograph of murderous little Huey Newton sitting in a large wicker chair, rifle in one hand and Batonka spear in the other, was taken in Axelrod's living room. "That's my chair in my home," she told me with a modest smile.

Betita Martinez—"When Cuba declared itself socialist, so did I!"—

was a Marxist with severe Anglo-Latina identity crisis issues. Her feminism was of the conventional Germaine Greer and Betty Friedan variety. Blunt and dismissive. These were women who sneered at conventional history for being the story of brutish "dead white men." Pretty well all things Christian and North European-American lay on the dark side for Betita and Beverly. Chicano race-conscious pot-stirring, the sort that lapses into ethnic fascism, was the dialectical leitmotif that kept it all together. Angela Davis liked Betita.

Martinez and Axelrod were pleasant to work with but extended trust only so far. They gave out their telephone numbers, never their addresses. They were two attractive older women whom I accepted at face value. They kept their politics under a loose wrap, there for the asking in snippets and casual drops, but nothing obviously on fire. Never screechy or oratorical. Nothing to be alarmed about. My political naïveté—more precisely, my credulity—had few limits in those times.

The other wake-up in the summer of 1968 and the most life-shifting was the popular reaction to the Vietnam War. They were all against it. Opposition became the only moral stance for a majority of students and faculty. Support of the war against Communism in Southeast Asia could hardly be said aloud for fear of provoking angry reactions. To have served in Vietnam had the equivalent status of being a defendant at Nuremberg. We were deranged "Baby Killers." These were insurmountable hurdles. There was no place for me in the anti-America chorus.

My combat service in Vietnam gave me satisfaction: I'd been in battle and not run (hard to do in a helicopter, anyhow). My boyhood waking hours were fixed on becoming a real American and to make my life in America. The yearning had been near desperate. Thus, I became increasingly contemptuous of my native-born colleagues who headed out of the country to avoid conscription, and their apologists.

That autumn I walked to the university campus with Lillian to look at the mob. We watched for a while until a young man fell to the ground in a pool of blood, victim of someone's quick knife a few feet away. I gripped

Lilly's hand and left. In a sense, I never returned to the campus again after that. At stage center was something alien and ugly and there was no part in it for me.

There was never a struggle over my political epiphany. No anxious soul-searching or conscious debate. I was and ever remain the traditional flag-waving immigrant who is deeply grateful for being allowed to open the golden door and enter. At Fort Totten, First Sergeant Curran told me, "You owe America." He was right. What did my over-indulged, pot-smoking, pampered American-born, foolishly indignant, insufferably self-righteous barricade-istas know? I disagreed with them all the way to the US Navy recruiting office.

While they let their hair grow down to their backsides and hectored against America, I put on a blue suit. The most marvelous experience of my entire professional life was the moment I opened the Navy Department's letter and read that my commission in the naval reserve was approved. I was in Taos swatting for my doctoral exams when the letter came. Find the nearest commissioned officer, the letter read, and get yourself sworn in.

No other professional gewgaw, medal, certificate, Attaboy! or hurrah tops the moment my adoptive country officially bestowed its trust and confidence by making me an officer in the United States Navy. Moses's bushes did not burn any brighter than the gold lace of that single ring on my sleeve.

The Navy

Full merrily
Hath this brave manage, this career been run.
                        —*Love's Labor's Lost*, 5.2.28–29

Anewly minted PhD in hand and a faculty appointment in the Massachusetts college system (1971–73) failed to bring anything approaching satisfaction. It was a bad time for Vietnam vets to be mingling in a liberal arts faculty. Our perspectives were mostly wildly disparate. More to the point, the prospect of a genteel campus life extending to the far horizon struck me with dread. Following a scant five semesters of teaching undergraduates and graduates, in late 1973 I defected into the regular Navy. My salary doubled.

In the days of mimeograph machines and dial telephones, the Navy managed requests for sea duty in an application with a box to check that read, "Any ship, any ocean." For a devotee of Horatio Hornblower tales, whose first book from Gloucester Library as a boy was *From Powder Monkey to Admiral*, and who loved all things salt and sea as well as any sort of ship, and whose favorite colors were blue and gold, these words were and will always remain, intoxicating. I reported to the World War II-era aircraft carrier USS *Ticonderoga*, with its plaque marking the spot on deck where a *kamikaze* detonated in 1944. White hats swarmed the Embarcadero in San Diego. It was January and people were watering their garden. I had never seen anyone doing that in midwinter. My ship lay across the harbor, at Coronado. Liberty launches ferried back and forth.

My office space was under the flight deck. Clash, bang, clang every few minutes, day and night as we cruised in the Pacific off the California coast. Watching mighty fighter aircraft perfecting touch-and-go skills on wobbling decks made me determined never to leave a carrier by air. And for many years I succeeded. Until the day I found myself trapped inside a Carrier on Board Delivery (COD) propeller-driven aircraft, belted, strapped, and helmeted when all my doubts were confirmed. Zero to 200 MPH in less than 5 seconds, coming or going, is exactly as uncomfortable as it sounds.

Twenty-six years followed, most of them in staff duty ashore and afloat with the Naval Reserve and on active duty. My first East Coast ship was the *Gearing*-class destroyer USS *Holder*, homeported in Boston. We sailed past the Warsaw Pact fishing fleet scouring the Atlantic Ocean of marine life outside US territorial waters. Soviet spy ships buzzed us. In Washington, I translated and transcribed U-boat deck logs from World War I, when Germans wrote in Gothic script, a distant and largely unrecognizable variant of the form we are used to. My grandmother wrote with Gothic letters and my dissertation had relied heavily on a grasp of paleography, mostly Elizabethan secretary handwriting, a nearly indecipherable system that gave way to italic. Because Italians wrote clearly, even in ancient times.

There were stints in the Pentagon, most notably during the two-hundredth anniversary of the country's founding, as Bicentennial Coordination Officer on the staff of the Navy's top civilian leader.

In a repeat of the D. H. Lawrence fellowship experience, when people complained that a graduate student in Tudor studies did not belong on the English novelist's sacred ground, a dyspeptic patriot grumped that only native-born Americans should be assigned to work on 1776 celebrations. (Maybe he thought I was a Hessian?) My assortment of immediate bosses, Rear Admiral Dave Cooney and Captain Brayton Harris notably disagreed.

Two stripes do not move molehills, never mind mountains, in US Defense Department circles, and close association with senior officials went only so far. To speed up favorable attention I resorted to the cheap trick of dropping "Lieutenant" in favor of "Doctor." There are not as many PhDs as you might think in US government circles, and the ruse worked better than expected, even when I showed up in uniform.

The most satisfactory result was getting some of the Pentagon's superannuated, peeling corridors freshly painted and respackled before their schedule time. "Make everything look good for our visitors," directed Navy Secretary J. William Middendorf, II, when—one of the Navy's Bicentennial programs—the building was to be opened to public tours. I did and it was probably then that the Secretary's administrative office chief, Commander (later Vice Admiral) John Poindexter—who also put a PhD after his name—heard that the work order initiated by Dr. Berryman was completed. "You mean Lieutenant Berryman, I think," he probably replied. Then he called me into his office to deliver a stern warning that military rank and academic degrees do not easily mix, and to cease and desist. The diploma was scarcely two years old and burned a hole in my ego. The Secretary was much amused. At my end, such shallow subterfuge still embarrasses me.

Bill Middendorf and his wife Isabelle and I developed a wonderful, personal friendship from that time forward. It has endured forty years, twenty-seven of those years as his archivist after he left the Navy Department. There is no greater trust than when a man puts his personal papers and collections into the custody of another.

We produced *Broad Stripes, Bright Stars*, the only recording by military musicians ever Congressionally-approved approved for commercial sale. Our goal was to offer a collection of American military music for sale to the public, in order to cover all costs of production and with the records available without restriction. But, first—because the service bands were forbidden by law to charge for live or recorded performances—we needed congressional approval. This was not all that easy, because the musician's union was adamant in opposition. The union feared a danger-

Advertisement for the only Congressionally-approved sale of a recording made by military musicians: *Broad Stripes and Bright Stars*, marketed by Radio Shack -- all copies sold out.

ous precedent that would take food off the tables of working musicians now and in the future.

At the congressional hearing, Rear Admiral William Thompson, the Chief of Information, made a clear and logical appeal for a once-in-a-lifetime exception. The head of the musician's union argued that paid union musicians should be given the job. Then the chairman of the committee called for a recess "to reconvene at the call of the chairman." The union representative—Sam Jack Kaufman—packed up his briefcase and left the room. Someone whispered to the admiral to stand by for a moment.

Lo! The chairman returned to the room, grabbed his gavel, called for a vote, announced "The 'ayes' have it," and the deal was done.

Coordinating the five primary Washington-based military bands—Army, Navy, Marine Corps, Coast Guard, and Air Force—was a tour de force in tact, balance, and mathematical precision. Everyone got exactly the same amount of exposure, within a margin of seconds. I wrote the album cover's prose and discovered interesting details at the US Park Service's Harper's Ferry Design and Exhibit Center library. For example,

British forces on the Yorktown surrender field were forbidden to play any martial music. Instead, they played a song called "The World Turned Upside Down." On the other hand, Washington's victorious army mocked the former enemy with "Yankee Doodle Dandy," which the British had often played to ridicule the ragtag Americans. The album was a sell-out through contract—a competitive award—with Radio Shack. We also assembled a "Bicentennial band" of musicians from all the services, that went on the road throughout the US and abroad.

Another of my projects was the coordination of Bicentennial commemorative coins for the three senior services. The idea for the Navy medal came from Middendorf himself. He owned a museum-quality collection of original bronze, silver, and gold national medals authorized by the Congress early in the nation's history. Designs of the new medal were shepherded to all concerned for approval. The commemorative medal became public law in an authorization by the 94th Congress, which also made Navy the executive agent for similar medals to honor the founding of the US Marine Corps (November 10, 1775) and the senior service, the US Army (June 14, 1775), when these services expressed interest in joining the project. (Founded in 1947, the Air Force was not yet a contender.) Hal Reed designed all the medals, and copies can be bought for a few dollars today from the Bureau of the Mint.

The medal's obverse depicts the Continental Navy's first flagship, USS *Alfred*. In the foreground is a Revolutionary War version of the Stars and Stripes with the stars shown in the line pattern traditional to our early navy. The anchor and eagle are symbolic of the sea and this nation. The reverse side celebrates the modern navy and its two hundred years of service. Nuclear-powered vessels are the submarine USS *George Washington*, guided-missile cruiser USS *Bainbridge*, and the carrier USS *Enterprise* with an A-4 at the moment of takeoff. Words are by Christopher Gadsden (South Carolina), a member of the first naval committee when the US Navy was born and who described the "First American fleet [is] in defense of the rights and liberties of the people."

The approval chop-chain was long and arduous up to and including each of the service chiefs, who personally inspected and approved the motifs, emblems, and design of the medals representing their particular service. The medals went into production in the autumn of 1975, in time for the birthdays. Artistic refinement may not be a US military strong suit. At best, the services know what they like—and everyone liked and understood their medals. A contrasting point of view soon followed.

After the US Mint had put up the medals for sale, the US Commission on Fine Arts protested. Writing for the Commission, National Gallery director J. Carter Brown opined that all three medals "were unanimously disapproved." He explained, "All three medals were unnecessarily cluttered, and the designs, which were hardly outstanding, contained several items whose precise meaning was not clear and which did not seem to be particularly relevant." The unhappy man continued, "Elements of scale, composition, and proportion also seem to be mishandled, particularly in the reverse design of the Navy medal, which might otherwise have been acceptable." The letter concludes, "It is this Commission's hope that the general quality of submissions from the Mint might be improved and that medals produced by the United States government might in future be something of which to be proud." His objection was noted and filed. The medals are still available today.

As the office's junior officer and senior gofer, I was tasked with coordinating details of a Bicentennial "jack" (a "jack" is the flag flown at the bow of every Navy ship when at anchor or in port). The "rattlesnake" version—a yellow-and-brown snake on a background of red and white stripes with the legend "Don't Tread on Me"—was another of the notions that came out of the Navy's Bicentennial Coordination Office, telephone numbers OXford 7-1775 and OXford 7-1776. Chief authority for both the flag's appearance and medal design was director of navy history, Vice Admiral Edwin Hooper, closely supported by his EA, Captain R. Long and the historical center's senior historian, Dr. W. J. Morgan. The flag was the more difficult project and questions abounded.

How many twists in the snake's body? How many rattles in the tail? Do the words "Don't Tread on Me" print on both sides? (They do not.) What should be the snake's skin pattern? There is no detailed contemporary depiction of the rattlesnake jack and anatomical details would have to be decided in-house. The timber rattler was favored because it is most common to the northeastern United States, the cradle of the American Revolution. Drawings were made and meetings held until a satisfactory, historically defensible pattern emerged. If our version was not exactly like the one made up by our Revolutionary forebears, they would have liked the twentieth-century interpretation, we believed. Besides, this latter-day contribution to shipboard ceremony was in itself a small but important Navy moment in its own right.

A brief pause in momentum followed fears by the State Department that the flag would be seen internationally (and domestically in the wake of the Vietnam War protests) as too bellicose. The observation was noted and filed.

Secretary of the Navy J. William Middendorf II presents a "formal" gold-fringed display version of the "rattlesnake jack" to President Gerald R. Ford.

On October 9, 1975, Middendorf presented one of the coins and a gold-fringed version of the jack to President Gerald Ford, a World War II Navy veteran, at Leutze Park parade ground, Washington Navy Yard. The president might have been commenting on our present time when he said, "I reject the prophets of doom who see nothing but depression at home and defeat abroad. I reject any advice to pull down the Stars and Stripes and sail home from the seas of the world to safe anchorage at home port."

The "Dont tread on me" jack proved to be hugely popular for the eighteen months of the bicentennial era, after which it was retired. It was returned to use following 9/11, when Captain Harris, by then long retired, sent a note to the Navy's chief of information, "How about bringing back 'Don't Tread On Me?'" It took about nine months to staff the proposal— about the same amount of time it took in 1974–75. Acceptance was just as enthusiastic and instant as before. This time, there was no comment about the appearance of belligerence.

Memorable in a different way was the proposal by a ranking intimate of Washington political circles that the Navy should paint its ships white and add the slogan "Come Visit the USA" painted on the transom. With his preternatural talent for minutiae, the Navy's Bicentennial executive coordinator, Lieutenant Commander Bill Eibert, worked out the dollar cost in white paint and labor, and then what it would cost to reapply the old haze grey color when the festivities were finished. The idea died quickly.

The Navy captured the Bicentennial by linking a planned International Naval Review (INR) with a civilian-orchestrated program, Operation Sail 1976 (OpSail), which invited many of the world's remaining "tall ships," for celebratory port visits, ending in New York Harbor. The result: a splendid spectacle on July 4, 1976, with participation by both the US President and Vice President.

Public enthusiasm sent ripples to old or dying waterfronts along the entire American littoral. New York's annual Fleet Week was born of it, along with annual tall ship visits to Baltimore, Norfolk, and other port cities. Restoration of Baltimore's inner harbor got its jump-start from the visits and the multitudes that came to see these great, magnificent sailing ships.

Early in the planning for New York the question was asked, "If some environmental zealot" got a court order to stop the event because some vessels lacked approved wastewater treatment plants, what then? The room went quiet. Most—or all—of the foreign tall ships did not comply with the Clean Water Act of 1972, including release of marine sewage from boats in navigable coastal waters. Congress was serious when it stipulated "no discharge" of either treated or untreated sewage within three miles of the coast. OpSail '76 as well as the International Naval Review could be brought to an abrupt, unceremonious halt. All of the Class A tall ships and many of the small Class B vessels belonged to foreign navies. For a drawn out moment there was a hush in the room. A senior New York City police officer broke the silence, "We would arrest and hold the person until the event was over. The city would then release the person and pay civil damages in whatever amount could be negotiated."

In 1975, after OpSail and INR plans got some press coverage, national Scout officials asked Navy for assistance to embark one boy and one girl from each state in the Union aboard a tall ship. The Navy agreed and OpSail offered to take on the task. Now and then we checked and were always assured that the project was on track. But . . . perhaps not. In mid-June 1976, when the final leg of a scheduled trans-Atlantic race was well under way and the ships had left Hamilton, Bermuda, for Newport, Rhode Island, I took a call from a reporter someplace in Kansas. "Why was the Navy going to disappoint so many young people after promising to get them aboard a tall ship?" he demanded. Did I have any comments?

Apparently, someone at OpSail had dropped a big ball and had not lined up any participation. That was news to us, but as Secretary Middendorf said, when Captain Harris brought him news of this potential problem, "The Navy does not disappoint young Americans. Go fix it."

The "when" was at once, on the instant, but the "how" of it wafted overhead, unthethered. Some problems can be solved on the elephant-to-elephant circuit of high-level intervention. Some are best handled from the deckplates as long as the messenger has an elephant-level remit. So it was that a hundred Boy Scouts and Girl Scouts of America plus about thirty adult escorts sat around in Newport, waiting hopefully for their ride. They'd heard the rumors and were pretty glum about it. My job was to reassure them that the US Navy had not let them down.

Except for the show of bravado, I was clueless about what to do.

Contacting senior visiting foreign attachés was no good. If in New-port at all, they had scattered to various watering holes throughout the town. When found, some were a sheet or more to the weather side of the wind. Key to a solution was the captain; only he could make an instant decision that would stick. Thus, conveyed aboard a borrowed motorboat, I met each tall ship as it approached the port, boarded, introduced myself, and asked to see the captain to whom I explained the quandary. No one turned me down. Germany's *Gorch Foch* was first to accept. It helped to be a Berliner parading about as a US Naval officer. There's a droll incon-gruity in a thing like that. Next, the Russians, *Tovarisch* (ex-*Gorch Foch*) and the old German P-Line grain racer, *Kruzenshtern*, largest of all the tall ships then still under sail. *Kruzenshtern's* wardroom smelled of cabbage. The ship had two captains, one navigated and did the seafaring and the other made political decisions. Both of them sat me down. They pretended consternation when we could not give them all 130 Scouts.

Romania was a lamentably poor appendage of the Eastern Bloc at that time, but they had the magnificent, purpose-built sail training ship *Mircea*, and all of us wanted her in the bicentennial celebration. But there were conditions to her participation. Simply, she required total support for all basic needs included refueling, groceries, and sanitation services. The Navy quietly agreed to pay the tab. She anchored in mid-harbor on the day of arrival and all seemed to be going well until some time after midnight, when I opened my hotel door to loud banging and in walked a contingent of five Romanian naval officers in full uniform, looking upset. I had never seen so much gold braid, not even in the SecNav corridor on the Pentagon's E-Ring, where my boss had his office. *Mircea's* garbage had not been picked up, the delegation informed me. The scow had gone from ship to ship but not to *Mircea*. The Russians were parked close by and they were laughing, I was told. The water barge had also not stopped. What was I going to do about it?

Still in my skivvies and with all that gold braid standing around glar-ing, I called the Pentagon's military duty office and explained the prob-lem. Then I telephoned my boss, Captain Harris. By 1000 that morning, the garbage scow pulled up alongside *Mircea*, followed by the water barge. All was well. Think about that for a moment. The United States is a land in which someone claiming the rank of lieutenant and speaking with an unlikely Anglo-German accent can persuade a senior officer in the Pentagon's watch spaces manned 24/7, late at night, of an improbable situation involving the garbage requirements of a sailing ship from an impoverished nation, and be taken seriously.

Lilly came along in the winter of 1975–76 when we sailed the Bahamas for almost three weeks aboard a splendid fifty-foot ketch that had been loaned to OpSail by the builder, Morgan Yachts. Three assistant naval attachés (from Holland, Germany, and Sweden) came as crew: Jack Kusters, Hans Katz, and Pelle Stenberg, respectively, and their wives. Arriving aboard in Florida, Jack announced, "I'm an engineering officer. Don't know a think about sailing." Pelle chimed in with, "Me, too. I'm an artillery officer." Pelle wore a t-shirt decorated with bullet holes and the caption, "Slowest gun in the West." Only Hans and the yacht's young skipper-on-loan knew about navigation and how not to run a ship aground, generally.

Outbound crossing the Florida Straits to Cat Key, our first port in the Bahamas, we pounded against the sea and were more underwater than on it. Hans's wife broke down in hysterics. When I looked in the cabin, Lilly—all of eleven years old—was flat out on the deck, unable to retch up anything more. She heard the hatch slide open, looked up, and gave me a little smile and a cheery wave. I was startled. She was no longer quite a child anymore, I realized. She was a person in her own right who had an uncommon amount of courage.

"Black ship! Black ship! What are your intentions?" I had hitched a ride from Newport aboard the Dutch-flag topsail schooner *Artemis*, leading the parade of Class B ships on July 4 in New York harbor. At that moment, a grey cliff that was the cruiser USS *Wainwright* bore down on us, dead ahead. The conning officer reasonably needed to know on what side of our black wooden hull he should pass.

Wainwright was the INR's presidential review platform. America's most senior leadership, civilian and military, were embarked on her. "Black ship! Black ship! What are your intentions?" the bridge watch called again, this time there was an edge to his voice. "Nic, you heard. Tell him what you're going to do," I said to *Artemis's* highly eccentric skipper, Nic Dekker. "Tell him fuck him. I only got 50 hp engines and I can't move as fast as he wants," Nic angrily shouted back. He threw in an alarming codicil, "Tell him I'm getting my rifle and will shoot out his fucking bridge windows!" "That's insane!" I yelled. But this was no idle threat. His crew told me that Nic had already made good on his promise in mid-Atlantic when a container ship, fully on automatic and with not a soul on watch, had nearly run down *Artemis*. When the container ship's officers returned to the wheelhouse they would have found bullet holes in the windows.

Furiously stamping his wooden sabots on deck—he wore these things underway—Nic muttered at last, "Starboard to starboard." And that's what I radioed back. Moments later I looked up as *Wainwright* passed. Everyone on her decks stared down at us in wonder. Noted in particular were Vice President Rockefeller's eyes. A remarkably blue shade of blue, I thought. Chief of Naval Operations Admiral James Holloway, standing with Secretary of State Henry Kissinger, looked bemused.

Centerpiece of the International Naval Review was the aircraft carrier USS *Forrestal*. The Ford White House had made it clear that whatever ship the Navy picked it would never, ever be USS *John F. Kennedy*.

Later that year, six of us including Nic and the cook, sailed *Artemis* from Fort Lauderdale to Houston through a gale across the Gulf of Mexico. A gale so fierce that it became necessary for the helmsman to tie his hands to the spokes of the wheel. The binnacle, original to the ship's 1903 construction, allowed a faint—a very faint—kerosene light to illuminate the compass card. Another Nic Dekker idiosyncratic marine innovation was a grand piano lashed to the cargo deck where he played his own compositions. All three of my daughters joyfully climbed *Artemis's* rigging. In port. Dockside.

The Beast on the Beach:
22 Tons of Maine Maritime History

What pleasure, sir, find we in life, to lock it
From action and adventure?
—*Cymbeline*, 4.4.3

A military career did not have 100 percent acceptance at home and in late 1976 I left the Navy to return to campus life, this time as a temporary, probationary, acting administrator with the duties of assistant dean of students and university ombudsman at the University of New Mexico. No less bored than I had been with my earlier college faculty experience in Massachusetts, my interests led to an adjunct title—no memory of what it was—with the History Department and the *New Mexico Historical Review*. To hew substance out of my daily routine of sophomoric complaints from callow undergraduates and dispel the annoyance of a fretful dean of students addicted to the incessant application of mouthwash mist, I began to write a series of grant proposals. Mostly successful, they took me to the world's wilder places and brought me immense personal satisfaction.

The adventures included the salvage of over twenty tons of a shipwreck now preserved for future generations to touch and smell and learn about. The project represents the nearest thing I leave as a monument on earth. It's a collective remembrance of which I am only a part. Many people were involved, any one of whom for any reason could have ruined the outcome. Or caprice by the Antarctic Territory's notoriously unreliable weather might have struck us down. Not in another thousand years can so many individuals and events align themselves so perfectly. Evils besieged us that came in battalion-size strength, but we were allowed to prevail. And now there's a monument.

There were two components to the Falklands Islands expedition in the austral summer of 1977–78. First, make a Silicone mold of the thirty-two-foot wide transom decoration on the Connecticut-built 1856 immigrant packet ship *Charles Cooper*, hulked in Port Stanley harbor since 1866. Then, remove a midships section of the Maine-built Down Easter *St. Mary*, wrecked in 1890 on Pinnacle Rock near Whale Cove on her maiden voyage, bound for San Francisco with a general cargo. The Maine State Museum in Augusta wanted a locally-built Cape Horner for its Arts and Industries of Maine exhibit hall. *St. Mary's* bones suited perfectly.

Both aims succeeded, though not without drama. *St. Mary* lay partly awash near Fitzroy and Bluff Cove settlements, thirty miles and eight hours away by spleen-splitting jeep ride across the "camp," as Falklanders refer to the land beyond Stanley. The ketch *Jenny Wren* (built in 1926) en route from South Africa to English Harbour, Antigua, via a glimpse of the Falklands, was chartered to carry the saws, chains, and related fuels and spare parts from Stanley. There was crockery aboard marked "Royal South Africa Yacht Club." We made camp under some low bluffs on the beach next to a gentoo penguin colony—someone reckoned there were 10,000 of the perpetually restless and loud little things.

Nearby lay the scattered bones of sperm whales that had stranded and died on the beach. Ribs six-feet long and empty eye sockets as big around as dinner plates. Major Nigel Willoughby's Royal Marine Commando Detachment helped with tents and arctic sleeping bags, primus stoves, and some field rations. *Jenny Wren's* three-man complement cheerily volunteered to help with the physical labor of cutting up the wreck as well as a hot meal aboard at day's end.

Legs of mutton hung in the rigging, cured by wind and salt air. One of the cook's recipes for mutton stew begins, "Scrape away the mould." For an evening's cabaret, the brothers delivered a repertoire of folk songs, mostly Irish revolutionary. Instrumentation was a cloth bandolier of pouches with small tin whistles in different scales. It is utterly unforget-

Battle of wits. The author . . . confronted by some locals. Falklands, 1978.

table to be aboard an old and elegant wooden sailing vessel rocking at anchor under the Southern Cross in a remote Falklands cove, the joinery protesting endless high winds, a glass of whiskey at hand, and listening to the sound of penny whistles keeping time with lyrics about freedom and "lobsterbacks." There is no darkness of the spirit so black that cannot be dispelled with the memory of such a time and place and sound.

Between squadrons of cormorants that homed among the timbers, we cut away a portion of *St. Mary* in ten numbered segments, forty feet by twelve feet to fit the museum's space. About thirty tons total were recovered, twenty-two tons of hull section, the remainder made up of the ship's detritus and miscellaneous spars we picked up on the beach, plus the *Cooper* transom molds. Besides making molds of the carvings, my job was to coordinate the shipping. The Falklands had not been on a regular trade route for about ninety years, making standard commercial freighting next to impossible and chartering hopelessly expensive. Dow Corning donated 1000 pounds of expensive Silicone and catalyst and lessons in how to make molds of fragile artifacts. Corporate officers support a romance adventure every few years, they said. The time before, it was a donation of Silicone to make copies of Mayan friezes. We needed a logistics bridge

Transom of the immigrant packet *Charles Cooper,* a storage hulk in Port Stanley habor, 1979. BELOW: The result of an ambitious effort to duplicate a portion of the transom, using 1000 pounds of Silicone, donated by Dow Corning, and following a technique already used to make copies of Mayan friezes.

from the US to the Falklands, and back.

Captain J. H. Scott at the Military Sealift Command solved the first leg of the problem by finding space aboard the fleet auxiliary, USNS *Mirfak*, which annually circumnavigated South America delivering munitions to allied navies. *Mirfak's* last US stop was the Leonardo, New Jersey, ammunition pier, where South Street Seaport Museum's historian, Norman Brouwer, made a fantastic last-minute delivery of our saws and drums of goop. Captain John Arens, *Mirfak's* master, waited for Brouwer to find him.

Arens wrote, "We were told by the home base in Bayonne, NJ, to hold the ship up until it all arrived." Arens also described how heavy seas almost tore away all our cargo. "You don't realize how close we came to losing your equipment," he wrote. "After leaving the New York area we hit a tremendous storm off the coast. Your equipment was stowed in the only available place, forward portside on the main deck. We had a hair-raising 4 days of continuous high seas and tremendous amount of water crashing on the foredeck and losing 25 50-gallon drums stowed aft on the foredeck. The bosun had secured your equipment real good because it was still in place when the storm was over."

Colonel George Maynes at the Defense Intelligence Agency alerted the US embassy in Buenos Aires where the newly arrived naval attaché, Captain Paul Barrish, had the unanticipated headache of coordinating arrival of our materials at the Argentine Navy's base in Puerto Belgrano. Rear Admirals Raul A. Fitte and Juan Jose Lombardo helped smooth the way with the Argentine Navy. At Puerto Belgrano, the Argentine Navy stored everything until the ARA *Bahía Buen Suceso* made her annual delivery at Stanley later in the season. Capitan de Fragata Contador Eduardo Ferro took wonderful care of our cargo and hosted me with generosity and much kindness, making rooms available in immaculate, turn-of-the-century quarters with spectacular ocean views of the South Atlantic, and food from a world-class galley. Eduardo loaded the chain saws and spare parts for the flight to Stanley, via Comodoro Rivadavia, in Patagonia. The Silicone followed on the *Bahía Buen Suceso*.

The largest extant section of *St. Mary*, most of the starboard side, lay flat against the beach, 130 feet long and 35 feet from the pin rail through the main deck. She had come to her end on the rocks sitting on her keel. Like a book on its spine, the ship broke in half down the middle. Three rows of deck beams pointed upwards, the main deck and two 'tween decks. Bits of her original cargo bound for San Francisco lay everywhere. Little brown bottles of Buchanan's Whisker Dye, saddlers tacks in neatly tied up boxes, and unnumbered cast iron toys, deeply corroded and bricked tight with sand incrustations but visible for what they had been and still showing some of their original color.

Cast-iron toy trains (January 1978) after partial immersion in the sea for almost a century; part of the *St. Mary's* general cargo, headed for San Francisco

Locals called *St. Mary* "the Christmas wreck" for the quantities of toys to be had. Iron fastenings in the hull were a constant menace to chainsaw operators as they tackled each section. The labor of cutting up the wreck was made harder by the unforgiving climate—winds of sixty knots and up and rain that could cut horizontally, playing tricks on focus, stripping muscles of their energy and endurance, and whittling away at our attention span.

Well into the project there erupted a terrific row with local authorities over credentials and licensing that came close to bringing the show to an ignominious end. The issue centered on the lack of clarity regarding team credentials and intentions, with particular focus on Peter Throckmorton who led the transom mold effort and, critically, the *St. Mary* project. Notably, there was an appalling absence of information sharing about the permanent removal of artifacts from the colony.

Whither the *St. Mary*? There had been no explanation of who we were, what we were doing, or that we expected to take things away from the colony. I was the only member of the expedition to have brought official letters of introduction and deposited them with Government House. Paul Barrish, the naval attaché in Buenos Aires had made a particular point of me doing that. With my military ID card in hand also, the credibility scale was tipped just enough to keep open a civil line of communication. The matter was aggravated further when Throcko, very drunk and breathing fire, marched on Government House to loudly denounce absolutely everyone within earshot. The colony's chief secretary (effectively the deputy governor), John Massingham, was moved to describe the expedition as

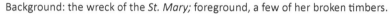

Background: the wreck of the *St. Mary*; foreground, a few of her broken timbers.

ABOVE: Call it, "leverage." Moving a piece of the *St. Mary,* the old-fashioned way. Author, in plaid shirt.

RIGHT: A somewhat more efficient method: dragging some timbers for transport to a waiting freighter.

"just the sort of persons we do not wish here." For the moment, work ceased on both the *Charles Cooper* and *St. Mary.*

Frank G. G. Carr, CB, CBE, to the rescue. The legendary postwar director of Britain's National Maritime Museum at Greenwich was a force of nature. No one could muster British VIP support faster or more effectively than Frank. Months on, when the *St. Mary* had come home to the applause of the media, Maine's governor, and its US senators, Massingham's letter glowed with benevolence: "We are pleased about the attention that we shall be receiving as a result" of the project, he wrote. "The Falkland's Governor J. R. W. Parker, had a very pleasant exchange with his opposite

The "rest" of the *St. Mary*, waiting to be hauled away . . . guarded by some locals.

number in Maine, and we hope that this latest enterprise—despite the initial problems—will result in a firm and mutually productive relationship between the Islands and maritime historians and others in America." He invited us back. Throcko remained persona non grata and never returned to the islands.

Once disassembled, each *St. Mary* hull section—numbered to help in the reassembly phase—was jacked up on to a wooden sled and skidded down the beach and over the tussock grass for more than two miles to the water's edge, from Kelp Lagoon to Pleasant Harbour. Throcko called it "the beast on the beach." The small interisland freighter, *Monsunen*, stood a half-mile offshore to tow the sections—they mostly bounced on the bottom—alongside where they were winched out of the water and stowed aboard. In the jetty, a gang crated and hoisted the cargo aboard the British Antarctic Survey's RRS *Bransfield* for the ocean trip to Southampton. At this point in the project the operation had progressed further than any of us really thought possible, but the skeptics rallied soon enough as circumstances deteriorated.

Returning the molds and *St. Mary* also hit significant speed bumps halfway along. As the salvaged relics neared Southampton, BAS shipping agents McGregor, Dow and Holland asked for a deposit to meet landing and handling fees. The money was needed to settle unavoidable expenses payable at the docks, to Her Majesty's Customs, and to the Receiver of

Wreck. The British taxpayer could not be expected to meet an American expedition's costs. By great good luck and some adroit staff work by museum officials, the Castine-based Maine Maritime Academy's school ship *State of Maine* offered to pick up our cargo and take it the rest of the way home. The ambush was being told to expect expenses amounting to $7,000 for pilotage, towage, and berthing. The *State of Maine* had altered its European schedule purely to accommodate the *St. Mary*. If we failed to meet these obligations, the cargo would be dumped at sea or, if landed, lost down an expensive and needless bureaucratic labyrinth involving hefty storage fees.

Our *deus ex machina* was Frank Carr. Again. Spiced with a passionate Welsh temperament, he flung himself completely into the project, pulling stops however and wherever he found them. Born on St. George's Day he, too, could slay dragons. If necessary—always with the nicest tact and apologies for "inflicting such a long letter"—his team included the residents of London's most signal buildings: 10, Downing Street, and Buckingham Palace.

Frank stayed on the phone or wrote letters on World Ship Trust Project Action Group letterhead (the WST was still in the process of being born) looking for solutions. Finally, he contacted Prime Minister James Callaghan, a fellow RNVR lieutenant in World War II. They had become friends when the PM played an active part in helping to save *Cutty Sark*. Working directly with the PM's private secretary, Receiver of Wreck John Medway was convinced that no action was called for on his part and he "tactfully kept out of the way." Customs could not legally escape being concerned, but they agreed to help and to charge only the barest, token sums. Their final tab was £10. It was discovered that the *State of Maine* was still owned by the US Navy, and she therefore ranked as a visiting warship. It was arranged through the Port Admiral that she would berth in HM Dockyard, Portsmouth, "free of all dues and charges." As an aside, Frank arranged for the *Maine's* midshipmen to visit HMS *Victory* during the ship's brief stay.

Colonel P. K. A. Todd, OBE, commanding the 3rd Transport Group, Royal Corps of Transport, McMullen Barracks in Marchwood used tank landing craft to convey the relics from Southampton to Portsmouth, where they were transferred into lighters, safe from all possible interference and ready to be placed alongside *State of Maine*. The BAS shipping clerk took infinite pains to placate the Dockers, a militant quasi-Marxist union that could refuse to handle the relics as well as deny anyone else to do so. In the end, the labor bill came to £328.04.

Lastly, as a fail-safe, Receiver of Wreck Medway helping to find the right contacts, the Royal Navy made available a Royal Fleet Auxiliary transport to pick up and deliver our relics to the United States in the event the *State of Maine* could not. (Plan B moved the sections by Royal Air Force flatbed truck to Holy Loch in Scotland, thence to Norfolk, Virginia, aboard a US Navy submarine resupply/repair surface ship.) By now, expenses payable to McGregor, Gow and Holland had shrunk to £466.

In Portland, Maine, the 1136th Transportation Company, 286th Supply and Service Battalion, Maine National Guard, trucked the pieces from the ship on flatbeds to the museum in Augusta, completing the final leg of a very long logistics transport bridge.

Paul Rivard, the museum's director, wrote to me, "*St. Mary* met with mixed emotions among our colleagues in the maritime museums. At the outset, many felt that the project couldn't be done within a reasonable budget and that conservation problems would be insurmountable. I am happy to report that all of the worst fears concerning the conservation . . . have proven to be exaggerated. In fact, we have as yet failed to spend the entire $30,000 awarded by the National Trust for conservation work." He continued,

> [If] you people did indeed cut the *St. Mary* section to the specification of 40', then I can say unequivocally that we did not see any shrinkage at all. When laid out on the floor of the museum, end to end, the *St. Mary* sections measured

just five inches short of 40'. Then the spaces eaten up by the chain saw cuts (and subsequently replaced in the installation at the museum) the total was an almost unbelievable perfect forty feet. I am convinced that the section we presently have at the museum is within fractions of the original dimensions that you took on the beach.

Rivard summed up the project and its impact on historic ships preservation: "I believe that when this exhibit opens, it will prove to a great many people that a very substantial contribution to the study of our maritime heritage can be made through indoor and outdoor use of ship fragments."

Throcko is owed every credit for the measurement accomplishment as well as for getting "the beast on the beach" (his words) loaded and ferried to Stanley. No one else had the skill or drive. I was mentally and physically crisped and Throcko was running on fumes, but he toughed it out.

Not long before Frank Carr died and his wife, Ruth, took to her bed in grief, never to leave, after both of their beloved elderly Scotties had died and Frank could stop walking behind them with bits of newspaper with which to wipe their bottoms, and after he could no longer reliably drive himself, they hosted us to lunch at his club, the Athenaeum, on Pall Mall. I warned Bobbie about the generosity of Ruth's scotch whiskey pours, and to sip slowly. They came all the way by taxi from their home in Blackheath. Cheery. Engaging. Utterly endearing Edwardians in tone and mien. We shall not see their like again. Ruth's lasting regret was that Frank never got the "K" to his CB. In a society in which national recognition comes from the palace (the process is complicated with an awards committee that sifts the merits and politics, but the effect is the same) these things can matter deeply. Sir Frank and Lady Ruth would have been nice.

During the follow-on austral summer of 1978–79, I returned to the Falklands with a small team to survey the only known ship to survive the

Vicar of Bray, abandoned at Goose Green, seen in January, 1979. The last-known remnant of the ships that were in San Francisco harbor when then Gold Rush began, 1849.

California stampede for the diggings, after gold was announced and ships' crew deserted en masse to prospect for their fortune. Only the English-built *Vicar of Bray* of 1841 kept enough crew aboard to get safely out of San Francisco harbor. The other ships are all still there, as landfill under what is now the Financial District and adjacent areas. The *Vicar* ended her days as a landing stage at Goose Green. The hope, never realized, was to salvage this literally unique piece of California history for an indoor exhibit by the US Park Service at the Maritime Museum in San Francisco, much as was done with the *St. Mary* in Maine.

Kim came along on this trip, all of nine years old. She arrived in Goose Green from Port Stanley over sixty miles and fourteen hours in a jeep across the trackless camp. In a climate that can get snow and rain on the same day, it is the wind that rules. The poor dear arrived under a layer of thick brown dust, crown to toe. But beaming, ear to ear.

By the spring of 1979, divorced and personally adrift but no less engaged with historic ship projects, I coordinated an expedition funded by the novelist Clive Cussler to find John Paul Jones's *Bonhomme Richard*, lost in the North Sea two centuries earlier. "Doc" Edgerton at MIT arranged for us to use one of the Klein sidescan sonars, a contraption for finding things on the seabed that the US military developed and he vastly improved. Doc invented the strobe light and high-speed photography. His cameras recorded the first atom bomb test in New Mexico, at the Trinity site, when a mock small town was filmed as it disintegrated under the heat and shock of a nuclear explosion. In his lab at MIT, he gave me a demonstration of how a rifle bullet can be seen to split a playing card in two. He explained the process clearly, but I never understood any of it, sadly. What is to be expected from the son of a German rocket scientist who failed the 11-plus?

Throcko accompanied us as marine archaeologist, but by then his confidence had weakened noticeably. Now that I am in my mid-seventies and less linear in my judgments, I understand him better. In life, he was a maritime version of Rooster Cogburn's character in *True Grit*, a bit of a rogue. Fearless and resolute and immensely capable, but also deeply alcoholic and ruined. There were two or three ex-wives and several children, but he died alone in his house in Newcastle, Maine, all of sixty-one-years old, undiscovered until a neighbor happened by. But Throcko left a legacy of well-written books, marine archaeological treasures fished from the bottom of the sea, and the *St. Mary*. His likeness stands in the yards above the exhibit, keeping watch.

The most signal achievement of our *Bonhomme Richard* expedition was to get a team drawn from throughout the United States to Bridlington, Yorkshire, and aboard our research vessel, *Arvor III* (property of Lord Elgin) safely and exactly on time. The twin-engine motor launch was secured for us by the indefatigable Frank Carr, who also smoothed the way with the Her Majesty's Coast Guard and the Receiver of Wreck (in case we found what we were looking for and wanted to take it out of British territorial waters). We went to sea as planned and combed pre-plotted lanes exactly as planned. Before the introduction of GPS-precise navigation within two or three feet left or right, the work was done by calibrating with transponders ashore. Knowing precisely where you are is critical for seabed searches.

The *"Bonhomme Richard* expedition," 1979. Expedition leader Clive Cussler. back row, fourth from left. Archaelogist Peter Throckmorton, sitting, far left. Author: bearded, sitting, facing camera.

We located a bomber that had come to grief in Filey Bay after a mission over the Continent in World War II. We also found a nineteenth-century sidewheel paddle ship, modern shipwrecks, and what might have been the cannons Jones jettisoned in his attempt to save the *Bonhomme Richard* (their density burned holes in the sonar's recording paper), but we did not locate our wreck. And in nigh-on forty years since, neither has anyone else during subsequent attempts, although they all came with vastly more sophisticated equipment, electronics, trained personnel, and resources than

A sonar trace of one of the many shipwrecks (possibly, a casualty of World War I) located during the unsuccessful search for *Bonhomme Richard*. (Courtesy, Klein Associates, Inc.)

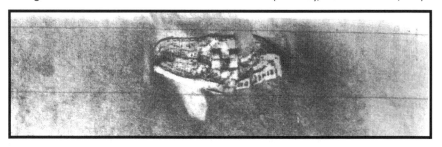

were available to us.

Kim came along on this adventure, too. The ocean does not agree with her, as we discovered on the journey from Port Stanley to Goose Green aboard *Jenny Wren*. But the change from wind and canvas to diesel engines made no difference. We rounded St. Abb's Head en route to Aberdeen with Kim firmly secure in her bunk.

The year 1979 was a tumultuous one, beginning with the *Vicar of Bray* project in the Falklands, punctuated with divorce from Judy, followed by the *Bonhomme Richard* expedition off the coast of Yorkshire. The girls were very hard hit. At the lowest moment, by the grace of God because there is no other explanation, I found Bobbie Truckey Travelstead, who was into a divorce of her own. "How peculiar," I thought when I was told, "Bobbie is the most unlikely candidate in my experience for a divorce. She doesn't look the type." Then, she put her trust into a professionally flattened, nearly financially indigent character who offered a doctorate no one was interested in hiring, a reserve naval commission currently not in much use, a green 1964 Dodge pickup, a small house in Albuquerque's South Valley barrio, and some old books. Asked why she would put the fate of her children, her mother, and herself in such as this she answers breezily, "I was looking for comic relief."

Bobbie's children were a little blonde-headed boy, Ted, who played soccer and baseball and Monique, a thirteen-year old copper-haired girl who made me nervous with her drive to get all-As in school. Even at thirteen, she already had the physical elegance, poise, and beauty that mark her into middle age. Ted is ever loyal and still makes us collapse with laughter. No boy ever grew into a man more dependable or true. Monique is good taste, good wine, and steadfast devotion. And I haven't even begun to write about the gift of her son, Max. In our sea and sail-oriented household, everyone gets the nudge. Thus, I managed to dragoon Monique into taking a billet aboard *Providence*, a replica of John Paul Jones's first command. She cruised in Atlantic waters off the New England coast. And loved the experience.

What Can You Do with a Drunken Sailor?

Our navy is addressed, our power collected,
Our substitutes in absence well invested,
And everything lies level to our wish.
                              —*Henry IV,* Part II, 4.3.

By 1982, I was long back in the Navy, now fully informed of the perils of becoming a colorful character fit for the pages of *National Geographic* or the envy of deskbound Prufrocks who can only fantasize about adventure. There were tuitions to think about. A fresh, wholly unexpected marriage to Bobbie to discover and nurture. If following my bliss meant being away from home for large swaths of time, it may as well be on military orders with a monthly paycheck.

I remember with deep affection how the skipper of USS *Comte de Grasse*, the flagship of a squadron of NATO anti-submarine destroyers, turned in the direction of Gibraltar as we headed into the Mediterranean— just to give me a closer look! And how it felt to make my first telephone call home to Bobbie from a deployed warship, Holland's HNLMS *Banckert* in the Bay of Biscay, having been delivered aboard at the end of a wire from a helicopter. When my ship visited Bergen, Norway, I was sent to Oslo with a checklist to prepare for the squadron's arrival: food suppliers, fresh-water connections, electrical compatibility between ships, and ceremonial events. The US Embassy loaned me an office.

Hoping to get the king's band, I telephoned His Majesty's naval aide-de-camp. "Come right over to the palace," he cheerily invited. "How do I get in?" It seemed an obvious question to me. "You knock on the door, of course," he replied. And so I maneuvered past splendidly uniformed military sentries and knocked on the palace door, which was opened immediately by a Norwegian Army officer. After finishing our cake and coffee, the aide announced, "Eric, I'm late for a meeting with His Majesty. Do you mind seeing yourself out?" I got completely lost in the palace but had a memorable hike looking for the front door. We got our band, horsehair-plumed helmets, and all.

In 1984, I had the job of coordinating media coverage of the change of command for Standing Naval Force Atlantic, a NATO squadron of ten or more submarine-hunting frigates and destroyers. This time, the annual ceremony was scheduled for the North Sea port of Wilhelmshaven, where a German officer aboard his flagship *Hamburg* would relieve his Royal Navy counterpart embarked on HMS *Glasgow*. The press swarmed. A German commodore with British, Canadian, and American warships under his command was news. Never, since 1968 when the squadron first formed, had the role of commodore been given to a German.

The officer so honored fussed that his naval service did not permit the wearing of a sword with his full-dress uniform. Medals were OK. The new German Navy had abandoned traditional ceremonial anachronisms like swords with their gold-bullion knots as being too warlike. In the postwar *Bundesmarine* the warrior spirit was toned down considerably. The US Navy—presumably, being more belligerent—made elegant use of them, but in my twenty-six years as a naval officer I never owned a sword largely because of their princely expense. On rare occasions when the dress code required, I borrowed one. As a kind of glorified wedding planner in Wilhelmshaven, making arrangements to manage journalists and television crews, I had no need of formal props of any kind. There was even free time for something else.

Back in Norfolk I had signed up with the Holocaust Writers Project, which led to a six-month-long taped interview with Shalom Steinbach, a survivor of the Kaunas ghetto in Lithuania and of Dachau. The result was published in an anthology of survivor reminiscences. Six months because

I wanted to know what sort of life was taken from him. Dachau was the denouement. What about youthful ambitions? How had he lived? What dreams? What hopes? Was there a girlfriend? Sports? Grandparents who laughed with joy when he came into their house? Eighteen or twenty hours of recordings came of it, but not every word. Sometimes the tape ran out as the memories bunched and crowded one another.

It was a sacrilege to interrupt, when Sol went far away, back to unimaginably pitiless surroundings. When the lyrics of a long-forgotten camp work song came to his lips, or the time he wept with helpless rage as his little brother was taken away at Dachau. Sometimes he was in a secret hiding place he called a *maline*, breathless and motionless, concealed from searching troops. Or in the railway boxcar, moving from Kaunas to Königsberg to the Munich suburbs with one family member after another ordered off the train until only he was left.

When Sol was so very far away in time and space I just sat still watching the shadows, and listened. His wife, Molly, would lean against the kitchen door and watch with me and listen, too. Thus, I learnt a lot about concentration camps and decided to take a Saturday away from the naval hoopla in Wilhelmshaven to find the nearest concentration camp. Outright death factories were all in Eastern Europe, mostly Poland, where anti-Semitism remains a stubborn fixture even today. My goal was a slave labor camp a couple hours' drive away. I went in the US Navy's working uniform of khakis and olive drab sweater, the least imaginable military organization associated with atrocities of any sort, never mind swords with gold-bullion tassels.

Virtually in the suburbs south of Hamburg, along the banks of the Elbe River, stand the remains of Neuengamme. The place was erected in 1938 to serve as a satellite of the Sachsenhausen concentration camp. Two years later it was given independent status as a concentration camp in its own right. Slave laborers, most of whom came from occupied Europe, were variously employed in construction (they built the camp), maintaining the Dove-Elbe Canal, and in the manufacture of ceramic roof tiles at a massive *Klinkerwerk* (brick works) factory shaped exactly like the letter "E." After 1942, the slaves were rented to commercial and industrial concerns throughout northern Germany. By war's end, Allies estimated that 80,000 had died.

Camp signage gives the number of dead at 55,000. Ten thousand perished in forced marches when the camp administration tried to out-distance the Allied advance. Several thousand died within hours of peace and safety when a Royal Air Force pilot, ignorant of his target, attacked their prison ship, the former luxury liner *Cap Arcona*.

Tucked deep amid farms and fields, Neuengamme is a difficult place to find. There were no markers or finger posts in the tiny village from which the camp gets its name. No symbol on the road map. Pedestrians were scarce on an early Saturday afternoon. The village policeman, a kindly soul, traced the way in the air with one hand while adjusting his suspenders with the other. Once in view, the place is unmistakably recognizable for what it had been. The Kommandant's villa, the old SS garage, air raid bunkers, barracks, factories, and remains of the concrete barbed-wire posts were all there. Was there a patent, I wondered, on the unmistakable shape of concentration camp post lighting? The spirit of the place, its *genius loci*, is in the enormous *Klinkerwerk*. Lately, a school-sponsored children's initiative had cut and bundled the saplings that grew against and through the building's sides. The former camp was remarkably undisturbed.

The same children planted daffodils that were now in bloom, and left pretty little markers to identify their class, school, and the project that had brought them to this place. Huge roof tiles, the biggest I have ever seen, lay scattered about. Buildings were moldy, disintegrating, and broken, but seemingly untouched by human hands. Deep green moss clung to crumbling bricks and rotting concrete. Signs warned visitors to keep away. There was a new museum with candid exhibits and memorials, but the original structures were left to decay in the thirty-nine years—almost to the day—since the war's end. No other visitors came to the camp on that Saturday. I was alone to listen to the ghosts inside the *Klinkerwerk*, clutching one of the roof tiles. Stock still, at the edge of the floorboards, listening. It was evening before I left my roof tile, the ghosts, and that long desolate silence.

Back in Wilhelmshaven where the big Standing Naval Force Atlantic change of command was about to take place, the hotel bar was mobbed. One of *Athabaskan's* Canadian pilots cleverly demonstrated the bear claw helicopter arresting-gear using brimming beer bottles and shot glasses. WESTLANT's Joe Brown was in high spirits because our chief of staff at headquarters in Norfolk, a peevish two-star possessed of a mind uncluttered by reflection, had launched an investigation to identify the source of a leak that he was being transferred. Good mood because the leak was true, the investigation stillborn.

An otherwise dreary, booze-laden office atmosphere in my part of Headquarters, Supreme Allied Command Atlantic (my posting) was relieved when my alcoholic captain called late at night from the Norfolk jail and Bobbie answered the phone. After explaining that he needed to be bailed out, she cheerfully replied, "Don't go anywhere, Stan. Eric will be right down." The anecdote became family lore. Thus concluded two years of erratic behavior, near constant aggressiveness, paranoia (fearing assassination he wore an ankle holster), and injuries severe enough to keep the man out of his job for weeks and, in the matter of stairs at home, for months. He confided only in the unit's yeoman, a junior petty officer.

In *Bugles and a Tiger*, English military author John Masters asks, "How much [does] the man underneath have to put up with, on his own behalf and on behalf of those under him before his complaint changes from 'disloyalty' to 'public service'?" The trouble is, I did not complain. I broke. Witnesses reported incidents of peculiar behavior during Stan's travels (he liked Brussels, especially) that brought investigators asking about him and his conduct. I deflected, defended, denied. The investigators went away. Stan was safe. At lunch in the mess one fine day I let loose with a torrent of grievances that were overheard and reported.

The truth is that I do not handle neurotic people at all well, and never successfully. Practice did not make me competent, even after years of trials with my mother. I try to appease, to distract. I play the courtier. It never works. At a military command, things do not end well for a deputy of modest seniority holding a reserve commission. So it was that I reported to the same chief of staff whose imminent departure had caused so much merriment in the bar in Wilhelmshaven. And then, inexplicably, things started to look brighter. The admiral's ignorant maundering and preening conceit made for such an aberrant occasion that my mood lightened. I laughed. Spontaneously, like reacting to a Monty Python skit. Out loud. The man's blather defused the situation, put the thing in balance again for me. I was grateful. He was bewildered and dismissive.

Not shot outright or staked out on an anthill, I was transferred effective that same afternoon and became deputy director to Captain Clark M. Gammell, a Naval Academy graduate Class of 1955. He puttied, sanded, replaced, repaired, and repainted enough of my battered reputation to get me a third stripe and brass hat—commander—in the next promotion cycle. Stan stumbled along a while longer until he stopped reporting for work and was found in his apartment in a pool of his own waste, his third wife long departed. He was quickly retired.

My own subsequent failure to reach captain's rank was due to a cocktail of circumstances and attitudes for which the Navy is entirely blameless. The collapse of the Soviet Union affected me deeply. This was the enemy I had detested all my life. I saw it as a monolith that would never be defeated. When the red flag came down over the Russian embassy in Washington, my interest in continuing to serve dissipated at an unexpected rate. Promotion meant an additional three or four years I did not want. My attitude went south. I had a penchant for being mouthy, anyhow.

When a one-star asked if I could solicit my officers for a contribution to buy a gift for the head of our community, a quiet demurral from me was not enough. I just had to express my feelings about the retiring flag

Captain Clark M. Gammell, USN. He followed the drunken sailor and rescued my career. PHOTO: U. S. Navy.

officer in question, and not in any old nuanced way but in words used by Oliver Cromwell to the Rump Parliament: "You have been here too long for any good you have done. For God's sake go and give place to better men." Alas, the one-star sat on the captain's selection board when it was my record that rolled up on the screen.

Other psychologically challenged officers came in and out of my life at inopportune moments. The navy's public affairs community, small as it was, seemed to have more than its fair share of unstable personalities. Among them a seven-times married junior officer with whom I shared an office, and a bipolar four-striper with homoerotic fantasies who targeted older women at the Naval Sea Systems Command. He lived next to his desk, on a couch. In the presence of an astonished admiral he walked across the dinner table to retrieve a bottle of wine, and walked back to his chair. It was a tell. Next morning, he was involuntarily placed under escort and remanded to the rubber room at Bethesda Naval Hospital. The admiral called me in his office. "Eric, you and I have a fine working relationship. I don't understand. Why didn't you come and tell me?" There was mutual trust and confidence indeed, but back of me was the long shadow of a different captain and admiral in another time and place.

The lesson for any hopeful future officer who reads these lines—also from John Masters—is "that a man must act by his lights and take the consequence, good or bad." But he must act, not run at the mouth in the mess.

I was brought into the public affairs community by Rear Admiral William "No Middle Initial" Thompson, the fellow responsible for the Navy Memorial in downtown Washington, DC. During the interview I made him laugh, and that did it. I was in. Following the retirement of his generation of World War II and Korean War veterans, some of his successors did not displace anywhere nearly as much intellectual and moral space. But it wasn't any of the spin doctors who represent the Navy to the media that mismanaged an historic press-related catastrophe. It was one of the best of the senior public affairs officers that lost control of a situation that careened to the death by suicide of Chief of Naval Operations Admiral Jeremy M. Boorda. The issue was pitifully irrelevant: it was about the metal appurtenance on a ribbon awarded to the captain, but perhaps not the crew of a ship in which the CNO had been a junior officer and had shared equally years earlier, off the Vietnam coast. The CNO was left unprotected by the public affairs community charged with interposing its mind and intellect between the Navy and the public. Public affairs officers who know better inexplicably approved an interview with an anonymous hack and self-promoting blowhard and the CNO. Before the interview could take place, the CNO, sitting on a bench at the Washington Navy Yard, pointed a pistol at his heart and pulled the trigger.

None of the personal reversals changed how I felt—or feel—about the US Navy. Plain and simply, I love it all. The ships. The men and women with whom I locked arms in common cause for a quarter century. The smell of fuel and bacon in the morning. The sound of a bosun's call on the quarterdeck, and quiet voices in the CIC. The color of haze-grey hulls and contrasting signal flags. The protocol of the wheelhouse and anachronistic traditions for wardroom etiquette. I met the likes of J. D. Bulkeley, Arleigh and Bobbie Burke, and most especially James Stockdale, with whom I share a perspective on the war we were sent to fight. How extraordinarily wonderful to have been allowed to be a part of it all. Why my time was peppered with alcoholics and terminal neurotics is hard to know. Perhaps I became a whacko magnet because my mother cast a spell. (That's a joke. I think.)

American Pacifism: Fickle, False and Full of Fraud

O, then, my father,
Will you permit that I shall stand condemned
A wandering vagabond, my rights and royalties
Plucked from my arms perforce and given away
To upstart unthrifts?

—*Richard II*, 2.3.122–26

John Berryman died in September 1996, quietly, with dignity, without complaint or fuss. The Churchdown Male Voice Choir came to St. Aldate's to sing Welsh anthems. Vicar Derek Sawyer officiated. "We'll Keep a Welcome in the Hillside," they sang. "Men of Harlech," and forever printed in my memory,

Softly, I will leave you softly
For my heart would break
if you should wake and see me go
So I leave you softly, long before you miss me.

I had just landed at London's Heathrow when I telephoned and heard John had passed that morning. Bushey and I collected Bobbie at the airport a couple of days later.

For about a year from late 1996, I was Special Assistant for Veterans Service Organizations, Office of the Special Assistant for Gulf War illnesses, in the Department of Defense. As such, on loan from my regular job with an obscure intelligence agency (later, a de facto annex of the CIA and renamed National Geospatial Intelligence Agency) I was responsible for close liaison between the federal government and military fraternal groups like the American Legion, Veterans of Foreign War, Disabled American Veterans, and such.

My scope included non-governmental organizations without a pedigree that claimed to represent veterans' interests, most particularly and noisily the National Gulf War Resource Center. The NGWRC's executive director, Jeff Ford, pushed for better treatment of Gulf War veterans who complained of suffering what became known as Gulf War Illness. Ford and I met often and worked together to address his concerns, slaying bureaucratic dragons wherever we found them. On May 7, 1997, he testified to Congress that our office—citing me by name—had made a significant difference for the better. Good rapport was not to last.

Others on the NGWRC's board had a different slant. Ford fell from grace for supporting the government's efforts. Following an intra-office donnybrook, he was ousted in place of a pacifist cabal that cared most about nuclear disarmament. NGWRC became its Trojan horse to insinuate an antinuclear, pacifist message. Under cover of wanting the best for veterans of Desert Storm—the operation by a US-led coalition to liberate Kuwait from Iraqi occupation in 1991—they blamed Gulf War illness on the use of depleted uranium in anti-tank munitions. (For reasons not clear, depleted uranium, DU, makes bullets super hard and ideal for killing enemy tanks.) DU is a heavy metal, like lead. It is the stuff that used to be painted on watch dial numbers to make them glow in the dark. DU bullets disintegrate on impact. Our pacifists insisted that when ingested by in-country troops slogging through Iraqi sand, dust from spent DU munitions caused their problems.

It was all so much political theater. Gulf War illness defied objective medical detection and definable, diagnosable symptoms. Troops as far distant as Guam complained of it. Neighbors of returning Gulf War soldiers said they contracted the illness. Wives complained of "burning semen" from their soldier husbands.

There is no single cause. There is no one illness—or a tight grouping of Gulf War-related illnesses—for which there are proven reasons or specific, correct treatments. Competing with DU as a single cause was ingestion of pyridostigmine bromide, administered to our soldiers as a prophylactic against the possible use of nerve gas by the Iraqis. However, pyridostigmine bromide has been safely prescribed by physicians since 1955 to treat myasthenia gravis, a chronic muscle disease. It was also argued that proximity to a large chemical weapons storage facility was to blame. By that logic, "a bit pregnant" makes complete medical sense. There is no "slight" exposure to nerve gas. Nerve gas does not practice random selection among masses of troops, but attacks everyone within range, permanently. The only Purple Heart awarded to a soldier in this context went to a young man who could not leave unmolested an aging canister of mustard gas. "Yes, son. It burns bad."

It was all hysteria on a pandemic scale fueled in no small way by a sensationalist media. Britain, France, and other Allies in the war did not experience anything like the same degree of reaction among its troops. In the US, complainants in the National Guard and Reserve far outnumbered all other categories of service. Men and women wrenched out of their civilian lives for an open-ended wartime commitment are bound to be more psychologically vulnerable than their professional, full-time counterparts. But woe to anyone in the Department of Defense who said as much.

As in any determined siege of the federal government by self-described victims claiming special needs for services rendered, the case is never over until the citizen wins. The alphabet soup of veterans' service organizations clambered aboard soon enough, hands outstretched, in support of their members. Lobbying Uncle Sam for ever-increased benefits is their raison d'être.

The chief NGWRC dissembler was a clever, ex-Navy officer-turned-pacifist, Dan Fahey, who waited to declare his conscientious objector status until after the Gulf War had started. Looking out for the NGWRC might have been an incidental interest; Fahey's real loyalty belonged with a San Francisco-based Swords to Ploughshares, an adjunct of the Berrigan brothers in Baltimore. Under cover of NGWRC, Fahey pushed hard that DU was to blame for Gulf War illnesses.

With Ford gone, I invited Fahey to Washington for a briefing by experts in the field of depleted munitions, military as well as civilian scientists. My illusion was that I could seduce Fahey with candor. Give me a list of names, I said. Speak with anyone. Ask any question you want.

We met in the concourse of the Pentagon and walked him to the meeting. He was pony-tailed, had a petulant look, pampered and sleek. His personality was like fishing in a bucket that hasn't got any fish in it. Militant activists are never persuaded by anyone who does not share in their belief. Not Maoists. Not National Socialists. And certainly not American pacifists on a self-righteous mission of "Give Peace a Chance." Fahey was guarded, taciturn. The afternoon was reserved just for his sake and he was given unfettered access to information and an open, nothing-to-hide demonstration. But Fahey was of a conspiratorial turn of mind and had long since tagged us as the enemy. When he got home, he excoriated us individually and as a group. We were villains from the outset. And in this vein he blamed us when he testified to Congress.

Bernie Rostker, the assistant secretary of the navy in charge of the Gulf War illness investigation and my straight-arrow boss, took Fahey's "facts" to task in a 2002 white paper published by the Rand Corporation, *Depleted Uranium: A Case Study of Good and Evil.* Rostker wrote, "I have defined *good* to mean the presentation of facts in a full and unbiased manner. I have defined *evil* to mean the purposeful presentation of facts in a less then [sic] full and in a biased manner. I have used the word *evil*, fully understanding its definition as 'something that is a cause or source of suffering, injury, or destruction.' . . . The story of DU is the story of how *good*, so far triumphed over *evil*."

At NGWRC's 1998 annual conference, we were paraded in the pacifist Tribunal révolutionnaire where the assembled worthies concluded

We may never know the identities of all the individuals involved in the decision to allow the exposure of hundreds of
thousands of our own troops to uranium contamination and
deny health care for exposed soldiers. These senior officials,
many of whom have been promoted since the Gulf War, may
never be held accountable for their actions. For posterity's
sake, let us acknowledge some of the key individuals responsible for the Department of Defense's epic disloyalty to its
own soldiers, sailors, airmen and marines: Bernard Rostker,
Stephen Joseph, Eric Berryman, Colonel Eric Daxon, Lieutenant General Dale Vesser, General Norman Schwartzkopf,
and General Colin Powell.

This is pretty good company to hang with.

I remained in harness long enough to see preparations made for the
invasion of Afghanistan and Iraq. I fully supported both decisions. Afghanistan because that's where the 9/11 attacks were hatched that targeted
so many Americans, including my wife, and Iraq because there was no
intelligence service in the Western World that did not believe Hussein had
weapons of mass destruction. No Allied country balked at the assessment.
None. The shrillest threat against us comes from the Middle East, and
that's where we must respond forcefully. Then comes China and the historic thuggishness of Russia.

Bobbie rose to senior-level staffer as a financial analyst in the office of
the Secretary of Defense (Program, Analysis and Evaluation). It was my
luck to have Jim Clapper host my farewell reception. I'm proud of that,
too. When the high, secure gates closed behind me as I left the compound
and its heavily armed guards, my life with secrets was done. No more
hearing about what might become a headline next week or next month.
And I am perfectly fine with that.

Bobbie and I retired together on the same weekend in 2003.

Waiting for God

There's no more faith in thee than in a
stewed prune, nor no more truth in thee than in a
drawn fox.

—Henry IV, Part I, 3.3.119–21

My mother and John made an effort to bring religion into our life after settling in Gloucester, actually going to speak with the vicar about membership in St. Aldate's. My stepfather's Welsh origins were plain chapel, but he identified himself to the Royal Air Force as Church of England, a detail duly recorded on his military dog tag. But it was mostly talk, no action. I tried out for the St. Aldate's choir but sang so softly that a beagle could not have heard me. Between St. Aldate's and our Boy Scout sponsor, St. Barnabas Church, there was just about enough attendance to memorize the Anglo-Catholic order of service and the Nicene Creed—the short version. I wore the Anglican identity like a small lapel button—I think we all did—and looked down on Catholics like everyone else.

My mother's idea of God lacked formal structure, but she introduced us. Christianity for her was a concept and mystery we needed to acknowledge. Church attendance was never integrated into our life. Hers was a secular, detached interest—closer to respectful curiosity than an expression of faith. We visited churches and walked in cemeteries as other people might stroll through the neighborhood to window-shop. My first memory of a church is an outing we made to a village in Upper Silesia, during the war. The church was little and displayed a portrait of the Black Madonna that my mother much admired and praised. Somewhere she obtained a color-lithograph prayer card with gilt edges of the same iconic picture that she kept in her purse for the rest of her life.

The card notwithstanding, she was uninterested in affiliation or regular attendance. The maternal side of the family is cheerfully indifferent. When her sister, Gertrud Grunz, my Aunt Tulla, died in Berlin in late 1991, a non-denominational spiritual speaker—I am at a loss as to his proper title—presided over a service that combined recognizable elements of a church funeral with pagan burial rites. He spoke nicely but vaguely of some indeterminate world spirit, leaving it to his listeners to conjure specific interpretations.

Mourners met in a place with stained-glass windows. It could have been a church or temple or maybe a mosque. The place was solemnly nonspecific. The rite of passage occurred several months after Tulla's death. The speaker wore a black gown and made a fine, even inspirational sermon, but nothing he said remotely hinted at a religion. I wore a suit and sat in the front row. He said complimentary things about the nephew coming all the way from America to attend his aunt's funeral.

A disposition of ashes followed the homily outdoors in a large, open, green, park-like landscape. There were no markers of any kind. No tombstones or bronze plates or sticks or the least little hint of funereal *stelae*, however discrete. Solemnly, a very thin man in a grey chauffeur's hat slowly marched the urn in outstretched arms to a small hole covered in evergreen branches. Observers stood to one side. Uncle Leo's ashes are in the same area, but no one could remember exactly where. We looked. Afterwards, mourners sat in a restaurant at a long table to eat ham sandwiches and drink schnapps.

After my mother's funeral service at St. Paul's church on Stroud Road in Gloucester her ashes were scattered on Painswick Beacon. The urn got an escort of motorcycle Hell's Angels wannabes that she had befriended somewhere. All those Knuckleheads thundering past 33, Conduit Street up to where a bonfire once waited to signal that the Spanish Armada had landed.

All of Germany has for years rationed the ground for conventional burials. My father's gravesite in Wernau was leased for twenty-five years. My stepmother, Ruth, arranged for an extension when she outlived the rental. When the lease ends, the remains are disinterred and disposed of in some way and the empty plot is re-rented.

The family conscience, my great aunt Sister Marie Barbutzki, life-long member of a Diakonissen order of Protestant nursing nuns. Before 1914 and between the wars she raced through her East Prussia territory on a motor bicycle. The last letters she wrote were to me. For no coherent reason, I came to believe that her spirit watches over my daughter Lilly.

Almost nobody on the German or the British side of my extended family went to church, not even semiregularly. Nor did anyone spend time commenting about the nature of God. With two exceptions: my great-aunt Marie Barbutzki, a Protestant nun who always included the hope for God's blessings in her letters to me, and my stepmother, when she was in her eighties. My father registered as a Protestant. If they expect to be baptized or confirmed or married or buried in a denominational setting, Germans must register their faith. This made it handy for National Socialists to round up those who did not measure up. The state reckons the dues and automatically subtracts them from earnings, rather like taxes.

Stefanie and I were back in Wernau-am-Neckar in late December 2006, about a month after Rainer died, before setting out together on our *camino* to Santiago de Compostela in late December 2006. Stef had nagged me unmercifully for years to be her personal interpreter on a visit to her Oma Ruth, my stepmother. There had been no opportunity in the days surrounding Rainer's funeral. Why it was my responsibility to answer this particular call I never knew, but persistent children will have their way. And Stefanie is nothing if not persistent. On the morning of our flight to Madrid as we checked the contents of the rucksacks we would have to carry in deep winter across the cordillera of northern Spain, Ruth came into the kitchen where we were having breakfast carrying Rainer's confirmation candle. It was a heavily decorated object, thick and substantial, carved and polychromed and in every way a fit symbol for the rite of Christian affirmation. Would we take the candle with us to Santiago de Compostela and leave it there, in the cathedral, she asked us?

Stefanie saw it instantly as a boon. We had been given a quest. At the end of our journey on January 11, 2007, we arrived exactly at noon as the tower bells rang out the Pilgrim's Mass and the cathedral's massive. We registered with the authorities and heard the priest recognize all arriving pilgrims: "And from America, a father and his daughter." Then the *Botafumeiro* started its arc to the ceiling, high above us. Everyone gasped in wonder and delight.

We told our Rainer confirmation candle story to one of the nuns—the cathedral's cantor, as it happened—and asked if we could light the candle somewhere inside and leave it there. "Come with me," she said and walked quickly carrying a ring of truly enormous, jingling iron keys to a tunnel directly under the high altar where a low, arched passageway led to a silver-and-gold reliquary. We were in the heart of Santiago de Compostela, at the source of what had inspired more than eleven centuries of pilgrims and reawakened faith in Europe, leading to the Renaissance.

Here lay the mortal remains of the soul who had inspired the most fabled pilgrimage in Christendom, after Jerusalem. The nun pointed to a spot next to the reliquary and asked, "Would this be alright?" Instantly understanding the significance of what the nun was offering, Stef burst into tears. So did I. When we left Santiago a week later, the little flame of my brother's confirmation candle still flickered dimly beside a vase of roses.

To make the pilgrimage we had hiked about 200 kilometers, mostly across Galicia—Hobbit country–in about twelve days, sometimes across snowfields. To obtain the cathedral's credential the minimum required distance is 100 kilometers, more if you're on horseback or a bicycle. The pilgrimage was my idea. After Bushey Shrubb, my old NATO shipmate, put the idea in my head, it wouldn't let go. Bushey and his wife Jo had walked to Lourdes using a donkey to carry their kit, and to Santiago with the same donkey, and when I heard, I was driven to make the walk, too. Bobbie was not so enthusiastic but let me go with Stefanie, on her winter break from the University of New Mexico, as my minder. In 2007, during a golden October, Bobbie and I hiked the same *camino* stretch. Once again, the *Botafumeiro* was on display during the noon mass. It's said that pilgrims get the arrival mass they deserve.

Here's some of what I got out of a long bout with cancer: It is all very well to describe oneself as being of this or that faith but unless the religion is put to practice, spiritual value is ephemeral. For Christian or Jew, hollow identification has no tensile strength. Most of us have no Walden Pond to indulge our spiritual breakthroughs. We need a coat hanger. No need to agree with everything hanging there, but we must have framework. Man or woman alone cannot build a credible substitute, however bucolic the backdrop.

Sartre's "Jewish inauthenticity" in *Reflexions sur la question juive* describes someone who is raised outside faith, traditions, or any culture that could claim to be Jewish. Sartre meant the spiritual tier inhabited by liberal Jews in Europe before World War II, which has its analogues in contemporary America. Indeterminate affiliation with a particular faith is like wearing a civic club pin—Rotary, Kiwanis—but never bothering with meetings. A badge is not enough. Tepid religious affiliation alone is a polite pretend, a "me too" during idle chitchat. A secret handshake. In the liberal France and Germany between the wars, what did people have left to embrace when jackboots come to take them away?

Faith means active practice within a community. Is that view too narrow? Atheists are generally scornful of a formalized faith, a belief system with "coat hangers" on which to drape a few signal rites, shalts and shalt nots. People parade any number of elaborate, perfectly sensible arguments to disavow the existence of God. Wonderfully educated and voluble skeptics adopt a knowing demeanor: see Christopher Hitchens and Stephen Hawking. Joseph Campbell's life-long study of world religions boxed him in a corner at the end of his time. There were so many forms, shapes, and sizes he forgot the substance. All is myth. Human existence has no higher significance, he concluded. In my century, Communism made it official that religion was bunk. They ground away churches and synagogues or made them into museums. The former East Germany is full of cathedrals turned into spiritless exhibition halls.

In more benign regions, people wear their respective labels and nod at God from time to time. "I'm Jewish. I go to services at Rosh Hashanah and Yom Kippur." "I'm Christian. I usually attend at Christmas and Easter." "I used to be Catholic but the Pope's views on women and homosexuals alienated me." The three main branches of Judaism dicker about recognizing each other's converts. Is Jewish a religion or a race? Orthodox Jewry—along with National Socialists—mark it as a race, passed along exclusively by the mother. To be Episcopalian in the United States means going to church dressed much as one does for brunch at a good club. Before the free-fall schism about ordination of homosexuals, Episcopalian was a cultural statement of class. Britain's equivalent, the Church of England, has given its homilies to ever-emptier churches since the end of World War II. People remember the church as the worshipful forum of their class-conscious masters. No one knuckles his forehead at passing gentry any more.

Why go to church, then?

At age fifty-eight, lung cancer introduced an overwhelming sense of mortality and I could no longer bear to be left spiritually adrift. I needed God and did not know where to look. Coughing up buckets of blood that morning, I repeated the Lord's Prayer and the Shema in my head. It's what I remembered. Anything would have done, but I knew only these two prayers. It was as far as my practical theology stretched. For thirty years I identified with the pure, simple monotheism of Judaism. I once wrote the children a windy, complex explanation of why Christianity's basic historical beliefs—virgin birth, man-god, etc.—overwhelm common sense. They do, but that misses the point.

All I had left to grasp could not hold me up. I had nothing that would help in the cancer ward at Georgetown University Hospital, spitting my life in to a blue plastic pail. There was urgency for more comfort than my reason could support, and no more time. A Catholic priest, Philip Cover, came into my room late that night. The years of logic over doctrine managed to embrace a love of ancient churches and cathedrals. During my one and only faculty job in New England when we lived in Ashby, Massachusetts, my former wife Judy joined in with my wish to support the village's old Unitarian church. The symbolic language of the early church in western Europe fascinated me enough that I once thought of writing a doctoral dissertation on medieval iconography, and I read and reread Emile Mâle, the incomparable French authority on the subject.

Bobbie and I always went to Christmas Eve services, sometimes even at Easter and increasingly more regularly on Sundays as we got a bit older. She, as a lapsed Catholic, and I because a moment of mystery on a Sunday morning suited me. I loved the beauty of an Anglican service, but it was an esthetic regard, like going to a concert. There was scant spiritual connection and I could not reconcile with my Christian foundations. Christianity did not make sense. If we dismissed Athena springing full-blown from the head of Zeus, how could we accept the virgin birth, manna from heaven, the burning bush, or the voice of God in the wilderness? My reason held it all at clinical arm's length as something to which I could not—or by education and training seriously should not—spend a lot of time debating.

So much head-over-heart juggling changed in an instant, and reason had nothing to do with it.

The day started when I stood hemorrhaging on the front lawn and Bobbie came roaring out of the house to drive us across town to the hospital, ignoring every cautionary traffic sign. When Father Cover visited my room on the first night I could barely speak, and looked as wretched and sounded just as wracked as Garbo's *Camille* in the last frames of the old movie. He chatted and mostly I listened or whispered cryptic replies. At the end of his stay, I asked him to return, to offer a prayer and hear some troubles before the surgery. "Why not now?" he replied, looking just a bit as one might when speaking to an idiot. I nodded. Phil went through his litany of last rites and at the end I felt that something very thick and crusted—a carapace of many sins—had been peeled away from me. And quietly and in a moment, I was cheerfully re-Christianized. Later, I wondered what the children would make of it.

Ever since I woke up and regained a brain in the hospital, it has been a continuing pursuit of life inside a Catholic context, within her sacraments and her wonder and to attempt to understand the journey and to properly meet its conclusion. Without fear. Dispelling fear is the challenge as well as the drama. The Catholic Church because it gives me joy and safety. I can't say why. Perhaps because when I was near-mute and loosing more blood than the machinery could pump back in, Bobbie's sleepy head touched mine as she muttered the Hail Mary. Perhaps because my conscience was heavy and I needed to say aloud what it was that so burdened me, and only the Catholic Church was willing to listen. Perhaps because, in my experience, the Church makes God profoundly accessible.

At her core there is kindness. Sanity is there, balance and calm. She looks to reconcile us to our fate every hour of every day in whatever mood, condition, or place we are in. She knows that she isn't perfect. Look not on our sins but on the faith of the Church, she begs. The politics—the weeds and frame of the dress—can be distracting. From the stance of having run out of time to debate the matter, the swirl of politics are so much administrative riprap and billowing clouds of smoke, like a dreadnought steaming into the line at Jutland, hiding the simple truth at the center.

I don't care if priests should marry or whether nuns may rollerblade or what there is to say for or against papal infallibility. These are all fascinating topics for people with time to spend on such things. I haven't any time. I awoke to this literally. There was no conscious weighing of pros and cons, of this and that. In the most profoundly literal sense I didn't chose Him, He chose me out of the crucible of the cancer.

I understand Aleksandr Solzhenitsyn's portrait of self-discovery in the Soviet gulag, where he is thankful for having been given much pain. It woke him up. When I lay dying on that hospital bed and was moved with the stirrings of God and the eternity that awaits me, my spirit changed so much I want to say, "Bless you, cancer!" At some point early in my convalescence, I understood that the life I lived before the cancer would be profoundly different to the life that followed. I had been spared for reasons I did not, could not, did not need to understand. Somewhere I read of an old rabbi's prayer—his fervent hope—that he would be granted a long illness in order to better prepare himself to meet God in the life to come. I think I know what he meant. I'd been given that opportunity early.

Chasing after more understanding about the startling new spiritual side of my life, in 1999 I began spending time at St. Anselm's Abbey, in Washington, DC. Overnights and long weekends. There was no regimen to follow, no course of study or directed reading and such, just the Hostmaster, Father Hilary Hayden, OSB, his community of about eighteen Benedictine monks, and Bobbie's marked-up copy of Thomas Merton's *New Seeds of Contemplation*. I had the unexpected luxury of a room with a wingback chair and ottoman to stretch out on, a good light, a nice bed and private bath, and the run of the kitchen whenever I was hungry. Effects of the lung cancer surgery the previous autumn gave me an energy window of about four hours between naps. At the Geospatial Intelligence Agency, my work schedule usually ended at noon.

I was welcome to attend the monk's routine of services and meals, but it was optional, not required. Here was a bath of intellectual and spiritual luxury.

Monks wake to their day at 6:00 with the cue of a heavily muffled buzzer. Sounded once for three or four seconds. Twenty minutes later is Lauds, morning prayers, followed immediately by breakfast taken buffet-style, with scrambled eggs on Sundays. At 8:30 comes mass. Prayers again at noon, then lunch, then evening prayers—Vespers—followed by dinner. All meals are in the refectory and eaten at long, plain wooden tables. Cloth napkins are kept in rings and used for a week, just as they were aboard warships when I first went to sea in the 1970s. The monks take turns cooking, serving, and cleaning up. They eat much too quickly. Last are prayers for the night, Compline. Some monasteries also rise and pray at about 2:00 for the continuity and safety of the world. Mercifully, St. Anselm's sleeps through until morning. Services are intoned, Gregorian, and lucid and often hauntingly lovely.

Silence is a rule.

Breakfast is silent. Lunch is silent, except for a reading from the Rule of St. Benedict and, maybe, some contemporary fiction or a travel book. Dinner is always silent except on Saturdays. The Lesser Silence governs daytime when occasional speech is acknowledged for the conduct of ordinary business, for phone calls and plumbers and such. Even at that, the routine is never to speak loudly and to restrict speech to an office or room, away from the hallways. The Greater Silence sets in at Vespers and lasts until daybreak. No conversations then, except for emergencies. Benedictines are flexible and do not lack common sense.

The silence they practice is not an absence of sound, exactly. Theirs is not an empty silence. Monastic stillness has something that shimmers in the air. Silences can be loaded with tension, anger, awkwardness, suppressed laughter, and so on. Monastic silence is an affirming thing. As closely as they live in community the monks give each other and their guests a careful privacy. Monks are not solitary bores.

There is a lively social life over dessert and coffee after dinner when conversation fairly burbles along. By tradition they take their names from ancient times: Father Aidan, Brother Bede, Brother Cuthbert, Brother Dunstan. At St. Anselm's, Cuthbert didn't much like his monastic name and changed it to George. George was not cut out for monastic life. Changing your Benedictine name is like showing up for parade in an Army uniform of your own design.

The abbot, Aidan Shea, knew a thing or two about the Army. "I was brought up in a marinade of 'should' and 'ought,'" he said, "and while the marinade did hold me in good stead, it did not seriously complicate my life.

> When I was young, I developed the habit of not reading letters until I had empty time in which to read them. I reasoned that if someone had taken the time to write me a letter, I was going to read said letter as thoughtfully as I could. Well, I once received a letter from the United States government. I hadn't opened it. Consequently, I did not appear on the day I was supposed to begin my life in the United States Army. Two military police went to my mother's home.
>
> She made them sit on the porch. She had no hearing at that point, hence gave them some 3 × 5 cards on which to write what they wanted to know. Finally, one of the military convincingly wrote that if she didn't tell them where I was, I would be in more trouble than I already was. The following day I was in the Army. And because Yahweh was not pleased with me, I wasn't sent North where one would expect someone from New England to go, but I was sent South to the basic training unit of the 82nd Airborne Infantry Division.
>
> The experience was a course in reality therapy for me, a world of the imperative. Early on in my fourteen weeks

at Ft. Jackson, South Carolina, there was a surprise inspection. Reveille sounded at 3:30 AM and we all "fell out," as it was styled. I was one of the two in my barracks chosen to be inspected. I had learned already that one did not look directly into the eyes of the officer; one simply looked steadily at something, which is what I was doing. I evidently was not paying close enough attention so the officer asked me if I knew the difference between a woman and the particular weapon I was carrying. I replied, "Indeed I do."

It was a serious mistake to have used "indeed." Very patient and very forbearing, he told me, in clear, Chaucerian English to pull in my stomach, push out my chest, pull in my chin, and snap my weapon to him. I pulled in, pushed out, pulled in, and snapped—and my weapon fell apart in the sand of South Carolina.

Why did it fall apart? Well, each night before one went to bed, one had to clean whatever weapon one was working on. We all but slept with the weapon. When I had finished cleaning my weapon, I had not accounted for everything. Not knowing what to do with what was left, I stuck a few things in my pocket. Among the treasures in my pocket was something about an inch and a half in length called a trigger-housing pin. Anyone would know that a trigger-housing pin must go someplace near the trigger. Because I did not make that leap in logic, my weapon fell apart. I received two weeks of KP [Kitchen Police is a notorious military misnomer for what amounts to indentured servitude to bad-tempered cooks in the mess hall] and had the most humiliating experience I had had up to that point in my life.

I thought a lot about that particular morning and the lesson therein. I wondered whether or not, analogically, there is a trigger-housing pin that I need to be sure to honor. And, of course, there is. What ultimately holds my life together is consciousness, and consciousness is often what I have stuck in my pocket, so to speak. In going from Boston to Columbia, South Carolina, I had gone from the marinade of "Should" and "Ought" to the marinade of "You will." My parents gave me strong and well-based Should and Oughts; the military gave me respect for the imperatives of life, "You *will*." the monastery and St. Anslem's school gave me the stunning truth of the verb "to *be*."

At the time of this homily to the oblates, Aidan was nearing his fiftieth year as a Benedictine monk and his forty-sixth as a teacher in the abbey school.

St. Anselm's church, like the rest of the monastery, is in semidarkness. Lots of electric light is expensive and unnecessary. From niches high on the church's brick walls candles flicker dimly. Choir stalls and pews are lit with old-fashioned individual overhead lamps. The church, like most of the place, was built during a ten-year period starting in about 1925. Electric illuminations installed at that time did not much keep up with the times.

On my first winter morning on retreat, the thin chains hanging above the choirs were invisible. All I saw were raised arms with open, outstretched fingers and a light magically coming on above each head. Early arrivals sat in darkness in the pews, hoods pulled up against the chill. No peril to darkness here. Soundlessness was a celebration. Concentrate. Think. God's voice comes in whispers and silence. The atmosphere of the monastery was serene and utterly safe. I had wondered about life at Prinknash Abbey, near Gloucester where I grew up, and now I knew a little, a very little, of how that life is lived and what such a life means. Thomas Merton and I, together.

On his seventieth birthday, Father Hayden sent a poem by R. S. Thomas. I have kept it near ever since:

I have seen the sun break through
To illuminate a small field
for a while, and gone my way
and forgotten it. But that was the pearl
of great price, the one field that had
the treasure in it. I realize now
that I must give up all that I have
to possess it. Life is not hurrying
on to a receding future, nor hankering after
an imagined past. It is the turning
aside like Moses to the miracle
of the lit bush, to a brightness
that seemed as transitory as your youth
once, but is the eternity that awaits you.

Regret, Remembrance, and the Whisper of Reconciliation

Taint not thy mind, nor let thy soul contrive
Against thy mother aught. Leave her to heaven
And to those thorns that in her bosom lodge
To prick and sting her.

—Hamlet, 1.5.92–95

W e were back in Albuquerque after a long trip to New York in 1970 in connection with the unexpected death of my father-in-law, temporarily at home in a dreary apartment on Pennsylvania, Northeast. I hammered away at the first draft of a dissertation on an Olympia portable typewriter, a vat of erasure fluid with a two-handled brush propped at hand, when my father came to mind. The suddenness and force of the image startled me. I stopped typing, looked at the clock, and instantly understood that he had died. The telegram from Germany came later in the day.

Oedipus never met my mother. Our relations were almost always sour. Here and there hints of an upbeat note, but nothing ever truly genuine right to the end, when we crashed and burned for the last time. Neither of us knew how to fix the problem. I was alienated but didn't consciously know it until late in life. After leaving home for America in 1958, I would sink out of sight for months, to resurface when one or another slightly abashed US Army company commander had me report to the orderly room to be told that my mother had written or telephoned or telegrammed to ask about me. I sought her approval and was repelled, all at the same time.

Following a disastrous visit to England in the summer of 1966, when the presence of an utterly enchanting two-year-old granddaughter was not enough to overcome her deep-seated dyspepsia, we stopped communicating altogether. The whole visit had been a shambles. This particular snit came at the end and was centered on something to do with a farewell dinner my mother had organized. Particulars of the disagreement, as trivial as they undoubtedly were, are long forgotten, but the upshot was that our invitation was angrily rescinded on the afternoon of the event.

Instead of our company on our last evening in England, my mother swapped Judy, Lillian, and me for her lodger, a large young woman who rented a room in the house and who earlier had agreed to do duty as that evening's baby sitter. We were left to forage. The next day, a car and driver were laid on to take us the hundred miles to London airport for our return flight to the United States. The scrubbed dinner invitation notwithstanding, and with no lightening of her mood, my mother came along for the ride. We sat in dismal silence staring out of the window. The drive lasted about a year. Still not speaking, my mother escorted us into the terminal, where I walked past the departure gate without a backward look. The sheer, wittering lunacy of the episode nags me. Not just a demented parent on a tear, but also the humiliation of being broke and unable to pay for my own getaway.

Some years later, my mother began again to make contact by sending packages of rare books and manuscripts. An autograph collection included Bram Stoker, Henry Irving, Lords Asquith and Balfour, and other prime ministers (cheerfully handed over for grandson Max). By now I had completed a master's degree and a doctorate, been commissioned in the US Navy Reserve, and landed a faculty job in the English department of a New England college. Slowly, cautiously, we exchanged pleasantries. After her diagnosis of uterine cancer, she announced a visit to us in Massachusetts. There were two more grandchildren she had never met. I badly wanted to introduce my life, the girls, our house in rural Ashby.

It was a long haul from 1958, when I had stepped aboard the *Zoella*

Lykes in Liverpool for the voyage to Mobile, to 1973, with half of those years spent in mind-numbing tedium as an army private (one of the world's leading oxymorons). There was also the other, epic historical contrast. An eon had passed since our life in wartime Germany, the chaos that followed the war, the starvation, and our frayed life in the England and Wales of the late 1940s and 1950s. My American life had turned out to be wondrous. I wanted to show it off. I wanted to shout, "Look! We have come through."

My mother and stepfather did not share a bedroom. Our house was big, but not big enough to accommodate them, each in a room of their own. Not without premeditated mischief, I offered her the study, a small building separate from the main house. One large, carpeted room lined with books but without a bathroom. We all knew this would be a final get-together. Her condition was terminal. Would she share a room with John and put up anywhere to see her son's life, his family, and her only grandchildren? My wife was unsure but I pressed on.

On multiple levels, it is a doubtful proposition for the child to test its parent. But what were my mother's priorities at life's end? I needed to know. What was my family worth? I toted a truckload of residual, suppressed anger. Gifts of rare books, antique porcelain, and pricey jewelry did not erase her dreadful behavior. Would she risk inconvenience for a greater good? I did not have to wait long. The telegram brought a terse answer: "Accommodations impossible. Trip canceled," it read. I wired back at once, "Mother impossible. Relationship canceled." Our last words. When mutual friends telephoned to say that she lay dying and to urge me to pick up the telephone, I did not. Neither did she.

A Victorian melodrama could not script a better denouement: she died on the day England calls Mothering Sunday. I was across the road talking with a neighbor about OPEC's extortionist pricing that rocketed gas to almost $1 per gallon when my wife came out to tell me that John Berryman was on the telephone. This time, there had been no premonition.

Death does not dispel unresolved family grievances. Death cements them in place. Dismay is fixed in time and space and for life, there for the asking in countless silent conversations with the deceased whom the living can engage as unbeatable foils in irresolvable arguments. If we do not speak out in life, we are doomed to perpetually thrash around with ghosts. If the parent departs unchallenged, the best we can hope for is a competent analyst.

There is metabolic relief. Time and old age took the barbs out of my rage. I stopped being afraid, though I still cannot look at an image of her face. There is no problem with photographs of her as a child and as a young woman before life came along to mug her, when she was in love and there was glamour and joy. But not the photos taken in my time. It's the eyes. For different but comparable reasons, through the many years of our separation, when neither of us knew about the other, my father kept an album in which he had carefully scissored all evidence of my mother from every photograph.

Because I refuse to cross that last threshold still pushing pins into her memory, I began to chronicle the good things she gave me. They were all extraordinary, quite enough to build a life on and relieve angst in times of dark thoughts.

I hover over my grandchildren in parks and elsewhere outdoors because of her and—Peter Lorre. (A child murderer portrayed with exceptional repellency by Peter Lorre in the film *M*, traumatized German mothers who came away terrified of letting their children out of sight. Horror is provoked in subtle, Greek drama style by suggestion: Lorre's shadow enfolds the little innocents ambling carefree home from school.)

I hike because she loved long country walks and climbing hills. I pick flowers, rose hips, and brambleberries along the way because she did. We starved together. We gleaned wheat fields after the harvest, picking out the hard brown grains to make a gluey paste that we happily ate. We set wire traps—never successful—to catch rabbits. We celebrated anything edible that came our way. She adored the theatre; I have been in the audience ever since. I take to museums, old churches, classical music, art galleries, and—especially—literature because of her.

My pleasure in schmaltzy Palm Court-style tearoom trios of piano, violin, and bass is hers. Franz Léhar on the radio during the war years made her heart leap. We listened together. I go to every performance within geographic reach of *The Merry Widow*. She introduced me to the tenor Richard Tauber.

Faith was her gift to me. Not the churchgoing, hallelujah-born-again-amen kind, but simple conviction of a benign God who is always willing to listen. She accepted openly, cheerfully, all races and creeds and predilections for glandular amusement. National Socialism was an abomination to her. She was proud of her titled Prussian heritage and loved Berlin and Germany and "our boys" in uniform. Her willowy elegance and beauty won her the attention of a movie studio and many interesting men, several of whom might have claimed to be my father. By temperament and training and especially by the *tsunami* of the Second World War, Ella von Wernen-Barbutzki was not cut out for motherhood.

When the bear had taken all the gold coins from her purse, denied her inheritance, and with only a smattering of education, beleaguered by poor personal decisions amid the chaos of war, burdened with responsibility for a child she did not want in a world gone to ashes, life became a disappointment to her that found expression in perpetual anger. I had Alecto for a mother. There was no protracted peace, only levels of irritability spiced with the suffocating possessiveness that only children with a "Mummy dearest" of their own understand.

In my thoughts today, she takes antidepressants now. Her anger is all gone. We are civil and speak calmly. We are rueful of shared, calamitous personal traits. We marvel at having come through. There is a kind of serenity. I thank her for giving me life and for the abundant inheritance that came through her. She embraces my wife, the children, grandchildren, and her great grandchildren. She loves our cottage and garden by the sea and adores a glass of red wine with my caprese.

My life came right in the end. Sometimes it seems to me that I was born defeated and thoroughly lost. But evil doesn't get all its way all of the time. Good hides in the chinks. The late-Penelope Fitzgerald wrote—with me and my ilk in mind? —that "not to be wanted is a positive condition" and that "every period makes sacrifices of a certain kind of person."

Being unwanted by a nation, in my case England, produced a fierce resolve to find something better. That turned out to be the United States. As for sacrificed persons, I am in good company. A sacrifice was made of our entire generation of *Kriegskinder*, but look at what we have achieved for ourselves.

"Was it worth it, Opa? Leaving everything behind forever never to come home again? Did you find your American dream?" "Yes, dear heart. It was worth everything. I did come home. It came true, all of it in more ways than I imagined."

The End

Epilogue

In mid-March 2015 cancer came back. Things hadn't felt right for a while and I wasn't surprised. There were over sixteen glorious years of remission in which we saw the children succeed and discovered we are hopelessly besotted grandparents. By coincidence, I had also come to the end of this narrative.

In one of my conversations with God, I asked why so much was taken from Job who had done nothing to deserve such staggering grief and why I, who had done everything to qualify being hammered into perdition, had my life restored. The answer isn't clear. My children flourish: Lillian was one of four graduate students out of a class of seventeen who stuck it out at UNM to graduate as a qualified professional who can test children for IQ (we have talked at length about Sir Cyril Burt).

Lilly is also Dayna's mother. Dayna, our nineteen-year old granddaughter, now on a full four-year academic scholarship at UNM after trumping college-level math, calculus, chemistry, physics, English, and German while still in high school. Her mother also taught math in the Albuquerque school system. Not hard to figure who got some of my father's genes. Monique, our corporate whiz kid who is more than qualified as an artist who could sell in her own right in any gallery, but became a senior executive in a major firm. She brought us Max, who was born with a huge sense of humor but Lilliputian weight at slightly less than two pounds after rollicking around inside his mother for all of about fifteen minutes. I think Max was fully literate at age five. Not a Lego contraption yet made that he can't put together using a concentrated focus that could melt granite. Kimberly graduated high school at sixteen. She has built a successful freelance writing career while raising our smallest grandchild, the irrepressible Moxie. Ted, who publishes books, writes plays, does stand-up comedy, and otherwise makes his life as a scriptwriter in Los Angeles. Ted had one moment of postgraduate ennui when he lay like Tutankhamen (but without the golden mask) on the front-room bed, staring at the ceiling. Until Stefanie stormed into the house one day and demanded to know what he was doing. Not much satisfied by his answer, she bundled him off with her to New York City where they shared an apartment in Astoria and launched into careers.

Stefanie Ilana was also born premature and fit inside a shoebox. She graduated with honors from high school and graduated magna cum laude in anthropology from UNM. Her degree was delayed by a couple of years when she volunteered to serve as an ostiologist on multiple disinterments to identify the bones of Union soldiers buried at Fort Craig cemetery, a frontier post in New Mexico during the Indian Wars and the Civil War. Relic hunters had begun to dig up the remains, looking for buttons and buckles because the soldiers were buried in full uniform. She is now a corporate executive with the UNM Fund. Mike Berryman, who will re-invent his world some day and make a success of it as we know he is capable of doing. And our lost grandson, Michael Greenstein. Come and find us some day. We won't bore you.

I'll stop with a Helen Corke poem, really a prayer we might have said together:

> To me, O Lord, whom thou hast made of slow understanding,
> unto whom all things are written as in water,
> unto whom all things are painted as the flickering of a flame,
> yet unto whom thou has given it to see the passing of thy shadow,
> and to hear the swift sound of the writing of thy pen,
> and upon thy violin the faint firm tapping of thy fingers, though

I know not its music,
give unto me one thing more!
Because that I, being sometimes but coward,
closing mine eyes against the stinging spray of thy surging,
fearing the blinding of the salt spume of thy flinging,
daring not to look upon the leaping of thy lighting,
yet dared to look upon Joy—give it also unto me to face
     unfearing, even Death!

Notes

Pages 1-10:

1/ Richard Wilbur (b. 1921), American poet laureate and two-time Pulitzer Prize winner. The quote is from "Richard Wilbur, The Art of Poetry No. 22," interview by Peter A. Stitt, *Paris Review* 72 (1977).

3/ Spyros Skouras (1893–1971), Greek-American movie executive who was president of 20th Century Fox from 1942 to 1962.

4/ Richard Wagner (1813–1883), German composer best known for his four-opera *Der Ring des Nibelungen* (The Ring of the Nibelung, 1848–74).

4/ Edward Bulwer-Lytton (1803–1873), British author best known for the opening of his novel *Paul Clifford* (1830), "It was a dark and stormy night."

8/ Thomas Merton (1915–1968), American Catholic poet, mystic, and social activist. See "The Autobiography" in Thomas Merton, *I Have Seen What I was Looking for: Selected Spiritual Writings*, with M. Basil Pennington (Hyde Park: New City Press, 2005), 22.

10/ Arthur Travers "Bomber" Harris (1892–1984), head of the RAF's Bomber Command, who implemented the British strategy of "area bombing" of German cities.

10/ Frederick Taylor (b. 1946), British historian and author of *Dresden:*

Tuesday, 13 February 1945 (London: Bloomsbury, 2004).

11/ Frederick Lindemann, 1st Viscount Cherwell (1886–1957) served as Winston Churchill's top scientific advisor.

11/ "The men hammered": Henni Krank, "The Operation Gomorra," retrieved April 14, 2015 from www.seniorennet-hamburg.de/zeitzeugen/vergessen/english/klank1_eng.htm.

12/ Martin Middlebrook, *Firestorm Hamburg: The Facts Surrounding the Destruction of a German City 1943* (Barnsley: Pen and Sword, 2012).

12/ Christopher Hitchens (1949–2011), Anglo-American author, critic, and atheist.

13/ Richard Condon's *The Manchurian Candidate* (1959) is a political thriller about a young American brainwashed into becoming an unwitting assassin in a Communist conspiracy.

15/ *Anschuluss*, the "union" effected by Germany's annexation of Austria in 1938.

15/ *Heim ins Reich*: Home into the empire.

15/ Adolf Hitler (1889–1945), founder and head of the Nazi Party and head of Germany 1933–45.

15/ Stephen Ambrose's *The Band of Brothers* (1992) recounts the story of the US Army's 101st Airborne Division's Easy Company from the preparations for D-Day through the end of World War II. The phrase is from Shakespeare's *Henry V.*

16/ *Verboten*: forbidden.

16/ *Schnell*: Quick!

16/ *Sieg Heil*: salute of the German Nationalist Party.

16/ *Juden raus!*: Jews out!

16/ *Achtung minen!*: Caution mines!

16/ *Hände hoch!*: Hands up!

17/ *Panzergrenadiers:* motorized infantry.

17/ *Gebirgsjäger*: light infantry mountain troops; literally mountain hunter.

17/ *Luftwaffe,* German air force.

17/ Hans-Georg Hess (1923–2008), U-boat captain.

17/ Douglas Bader (1910–1982), British flying ace despite having lost his legs in a prewar aerial acrobatics accident.

17/ Erich Hartmann, "the Black Devil" (1922–1993), the most successful fighter ace in history, credited with downing 352 aircraft—345 Russian, 7 American.

17/ *Kormoran* was a German commerce raider commanded by Theodor Detmers (1902–1976).

17/ Horatio Lord Nelson (1758–1805) was a British admiral most celebrated for his victory at the battle of Trafalgar in 1805.

17/ Erwin Rommel, "the Desert Fox" (1891–1944), German field marshal and tank commander who commanded the Afrika Korps.

17/ Heinz Guderian (1888–1954), German general and tank commander.

17/ Gerd von Rundstedt (1875–1953), German field marshall.

17/ Fridolin von Senger und Etterlin (1891–1963), general and tank commander.

17/ Kurt "Panzer" Meyer (1910–1961), Waffen-SS tank general.

17/ Michael Wittmann (1914–1944), Waffen-SS tank captain.

18/ 1MC: 1 Main Circuit, the shipboard public address system on US Navy vessels

18/ Gerhard "Gerd" Thäter (1916–2004), U-boat captain.

19/ *Kriegsmarine*: German navy during World War II.

19/ *Wehrmacht:* German army in World War II.

20/ Vladimir Lenin (1870–1924), first leader of the Soviet Union.

20 /Ernesto "Che" Guevara (1928–1967), Argentine doctor and revolutionary.

20/ Heinrich Böll (1917–1985), Nobel Prize-winning German author.

20/ Günther Grass (1927–2015), Nobel Prize-winning German author. After his application to join the submarine service was declined, in late 1944 he was drafted into an SS Panzer Division, a fact he did not reveal publicly until 2006.

20/ *SS: Schutzstaffel* (protection squadron), the armed wing of the Nazi Party. The Waffen-SS were frontline troops nominally independent of the Wehrmacht and with a different rank system. Other formations served as Hitler's bodyguard and ran the concentration camp system.

20 / Horst Tappert (1923–2008), German movie and television actor.

20/ *Infanterie, Flak, oder SS:* Infantry, anti-aircraft battery, or SS.

21/ *Bundesmarine*: postwar German navy.

21/ Wound Badge (*Verwundetenabzeichen*) was awarded to soldiers, and towards the end of World War II, civilians.

21/ Iron Cross, military decoration, introduced in 1813, awarded for acts of bravery, heroism, and leadership.

21/ The Pour le Mérite (French "For merit"), known informally as the Blue Max (German *Blauer Max*); decoration awarded for extraordinary personal achievement, introduced in 1740.

21/ *Vae Victis*: "Woe to the vanquished" (Latin).

23/ Guy Penrose Gibson (1918–1944), RAF wing commander who led Operation Chastise against the Möhne and Eder Dams in the Ruhr Valley.

23/ Victoria Cross (VC), highest military decoration awarded for valour "in the face of the enemy" to members of the armed forces throughout the British Empire.

23/ Distinguished Service Order (DSO), military decoration awarded "for distinguished services during active operations against the enemy." A Bar is added to this and the DFC for subsequent acts of such leadership.

23/ Distinguished Flying Cross (DFC), military decoration awarded to personnel of the RAF and other services for "an act or acts of valour, courage or devotion to duty whilst flying in active operations against the enemy."

23/ *The Cockleshell Heroes* (1955), fictionalised account of a December 1942 raid by British commandos who attacked shipping in Bordeaux, France, from collapsible canoes.

24/ *The Young Lions* (1958) was based on Irwin Shaw's 1948 novel of the same name.

24/ Erich von Stroheim (1885–1957), Austrian-American actor-director.

24/ Marlene Dietrich (1901–1992), German-American actress and singer.

24/ Manfred von Richthofen, "the Red Baron" (1892–1918), was a World War I flying ace who remains one of the best-known fighter pilots in the world.

24/ Lothar von Arnauld de la Perière (1886–1941), was the most successful submarine ace of World War I, or ever.

24/ Erich Maria Remarque, a German veteran of World War I, published *All Quiet on the Western Front (Im Westen nichts Neues)* in 1929. It was made into a Hollywood movie in 1930.

24/ *La Grand Illusion* (1937) by French director Jean Renoir, depicts a group of French POWs during World War I.

25/ *The Greatest Generation* is the title of a 1997 book by journalist Tom Brokaw, who used it to describe the Americans who grew up in the Great Depression, fought in World War II because "it was the right thing to do," and contributed to America's postwar prosperity.

25/ *The Dirty Dozen* (1967) is a film about a group of twelve convicts chosen to carry out a suicide mission: to capture high-ranking German officers before the D-Day invasion.

25/ *Inglourious Basterds* (2009), directed by Quentin Tarantino, was a German-American production involving a successful plot to kill Hitler at a movie premiere.

25/ Cornelius Ryan's *The Longest Day* (1959) and *A Bridge Too Far* (1970) recounted the stories of the D-Day invasion and the subsequent failure of Operation Market Garden in the Netherlands, respectively.

25/ Steven Spielberg's movie *Saving Private Ryan* (1998) is the fictional story of a group of soldiers who penetrate enemy lines after D-Day to rescue a paratrooper.

25/ "Memphis Belle" was a B-17 Flying Fortress whose aircrew was the first in the US Eighth Air Force to complete 25 missions in Europe and return to the United States. They were the subject of a 1944 documentary and a 1990 film.

25/ *Schindler's List* (1993), directed by Steven Spielberg, movie based on

Thomas Keneally's 1982 book, Schindler's Ark, about Oskar Schindler, a German businessman who saved the lives of more than a thousand Jews employed in his factories during World War II.

25/ Treblinka and Sobibór were extermination camps, and Auschwitz-Birkenau included concentration, extermination, and labor camps; all were located in what is now Poland.

25/ *Herrenvolk*: master race; a form of democracy in which ethnic minorities are disenfranchised.

25/ *St. Louis:* In May 1939, the German government allowed 933 Jews to leave Germany aboard the passenger ship *St. Louis.* Denied entry to Cuba or the United States, the ship sailed for Antwerp. Some of the passengers remained in Belgium, while others went to France, the Netherlands, and Britain.

26/ The Locarno Treaties (1925) were intended to secure peace in Europe by guaranteeing postwar borders.

28/ Richard Tauber (1891–1948), Austrian tenor of Jewish ancestry who settled in England during World War II.

28/ Werner von Braun (1912–1977), German aerospace engineer who later headed NASA's Saturn rocket program and was thereby instrumental in getting spacecraft to the moon.

28/ Cape Story by the Sea is a neighborhood of Virginia Beach, Virginia.

31/ Doodlebugs was another British nickname for Buzz Bombs.

33/ Christopher Isherwood (1904–1986), Anglo-American author whose books include *Berlin Stories* (1945).

33/ Ernst Udet (1896-1941), World War I flying ace and Luftwaffe general in World War II; he died a suicide.

37/ Wannsee: The westernmost part of Berlin.

39/ Langenbrück: After 1945 renamed Mostowice and ceded to Poland, along with most of Silesia

39/ P. G. Wodehouse (1881–1975), Anglo-American author most famous for his characters the hapless Bertie Wooster and his longsuffering manservant, Jeeves.

46/ "Lili Marleen": song based on a poem by Hans Leip (1893–1983) and popular among both Axis and Allied soldiers during World War II.

48/ James Fenimore Cooper (1789–1851), American novelist whose four *Leatherstocking* novels include *The Last of the Mohicans* (1826) and *The Deerslayer* (1841), featuring backwoodsman Natty Bumppo and Delaware Indian chief Chingachgook.

56/ Ian Buruma, *Year Zero: A History of 1945* (New York: Penguin Press, 2013).

61/ Godwin's Law: http://en.wikipedia.org/wiki/Godwin%27s_law.

61/ "my book," Eric Dietrich-Berryman, Charlotte Hammond, and R. E. White, *Passport Not Required: U.S. Volunteers in the Royal Navy, 1939–1941* (Annapolis: Naval Institute Press, 2010).

62/ P. D. Wren's novel *Beau Geste* (1924) recounts the adventures of the three upper-class English Geste brothers; the French title means "gracious gesture."

63/ "Shoulder the sky": A. E. Housman, *Last Poems*, IX.

63/ The Pergamonmuseum, opened in Berlin in 1907, remains one of the world's great museums.

65/ Hermann Göring (1893–1946), close ally of Hitler and head of the Luftwaffe.

65/ "when Roosevelt": in Herbert Hoover, *Freedom Betrayed: Herbert Hoover's Secret History of the Second World War and Its Aftermath,* edited by George H. Nash (Stanford: Hoover Institution Press, 2011).

66/ "The anti-Semitic feeling": A. Lawrence Lowell, letter in the New York Times June 17, 1922, p. 1.

66/ "to improve the race": Charles B. Davenport, *Heredity in Relation to Eugenics* (New York: Henry Holt, 1911).

72/ SCI (sensitive compartmented information), an intelligence classification above top secret.

73/ Jennifer V. Evans, *Life Among the Ruins: Cityscape and Sexuality in Cold War Berlin* (Basingstoke: Palgrave Macmillan, 2011).

73/ Henry Morgenthau, Jr. (1891–1967), Roosevelt's Secretary of the Treasury, forced a strict interpretation of Joint Chiefs of Staff directive JCS 1067 in the economic and nutritional governance of Occupied Germany. Strong practical and moral objections by senior and military officials replaced JCS 1067 with JCS 1779, which urged that a prosperous postwar Europe required an economically stable and productive Germany.

74/ David Irving (b. 1938), English writer and Holocaust denier.

74/ Lucius D. Clay (1897–1978), American deputy military governor of Occupied Germany, beloved especially by Berliners for his fairness and administrative genius.

75/ Harry Dexter White (1892–1948) was a prominent economist who passed secrets to the Soviet Union during and after the war. He died of a heart attack shortly after testifying before the House Un-American Activities Committee.

75/ Rhondda Valley: The coalmining region of South Wales—poor in material luxuries, especially in 1947.

84/ Poppy Day: An alternative name for Remembrance Day (originally Armistice Day), which commemorates the end of World War I "at the 11th hour of the 11th day of the 11th month" in 1918. The red poppy was chosen to symbolize the dead after John McCrae's celebrated 1915 poem, which begins "In Flanders fields the poppies blow."

85/ David Lloyd George (1863–1945), prime minister of the United Kingdom, 1916–22.

85/ Basil Henry Liddell-Hart (1895–1970), soldier and military historian.

85/ T. E. Lawrence (1888–1935), archaeologist, soldier, and author, known as Lawrence of Arabia for his exploits in World War I.

85/ Field Marshall Edmund Allenby (1861–1936), commander of the British Egyptian Expeditionary Force in World War I.

85/ Winston Churchill (1874–1965), author, historian, and prime minister of the UK, 1940–45 and 1951–55.

85/ Cyril Burt (1883–1971), educational psychologist.

87/ Bob Cratchit, Ebenezer Scrooge's underpaid clerk in Charles Dickens's *A Christmas Carol* (1843).

87/ Secondary Modern: Under Britain's tripartite education system, in place from 1944 to the 1970s, Secondary Modern Schools were high schools for students not deemed fit for either academic or vocational education.

87/ *The Admirable Crichton* (1902) is a comedy written by J. M. Barrie.

87/ *Upstairs, Downstairs,* 1970s British television drama set in a large house in London between 1903 and 1930.

87/ *Downton Abbey*, 2010s British television drama set in a Yorkshire country house starting in 1912.

87/ From John O'Groats to Land's End: from one end (in Cornwall) of Great Britain to the other (in Scotland).

88/ James Agee (1909–1955), American author best known for *Let Us Now Praise Famous Men*, an inquiry into the conditions of southern sharecroppers during the Dust Bowl of the 1930s.

88/ *Shudra*: the lowest of the four castes in Hinduism.

88/ Helen Corke (1882–1978), English teacher and writer, and one-time colleague of novelist and poet D. H. Lawrence.

90/ Alfred Rosenberg (1893–1946), Hitler's Commissar for the Supervision of Intellectual and Ideological Education of the Nazi Party, executed for war crimes.

90/ *Ahnenforschung*: genealogy.

90/ *Untermenschen*: inferior people; literally, "sub-humans."

90/ *The Cruel Sea* (1951) recounts the lives and exploits of sailors serving in Royal Navy corvettes during the Battle of the Atlantic.

91/ *Simplicissimus* was published from 1896 to 1967, except from 1944 to 1954.

91/ Kuttel Daddeldu was a sailor who first appeared in Joachim Ringelnatz's *Vom Seemann Kuttel Daddeldu* (1920).

91/ In 1906, Friedrich Wilhelm Voigt (1849–1922) posed as a military officer and, with a number of soldiers under his command, arrested the mayor and treasurer of Köpenick (near Berlin) for malfeasance and seized more than 4,000 marks from the municipal treasury. Arrested and sentenced to jail, he was later pardoned by Kaiser Wilhelm II. Carl Zuckmayer's play, *The Captain of Köpenick* (1931), was the first of many theatrical and cinematic retellings, and as recently as 2006, the German post office issued a stamp depicting Der Hauptmann von Köpenick.

91/ Father Arnell and Stephen Dedalus are characters in James Joyce's autobiographical novel, *A Portrait of the Artist as a Young Man* (1916).

92/ *The Tin Drum (Die Blechtrommel,* 1959) is the first novel in Grass's Danzig Trilogy.

92/ Dogberry: self-important constable in William Shakespeare's *Much Ado about Nothing.*

92/ Mrs. Malaprop: a misspoken character in Richard Brinsley Sheridan's comedy *The Rivals* (1775).

92/ Neddie Seagoon: a gullible fool on *The Goon Show*, a 1950s British TV comedy starring Spike Milligan, Peter Sellers, and others.

92/ *The Dandy* was published from 1937 to 2012, *Film Fun* from 1920 to 1962, and *Eagle* from 1950 to 1969.

92/ Biggles: Nickname of James Bigglesworth, fictional pilot and adventurer of the Biggles series of adventure books written by W. E. Johns (1893–1968).

92/ Wilfred Pickles (1904–1978), the first BBC radio announcer to speak in a regional accent rather than the BBC's Received Pronunciation.

92/ Bud Flanagan (1896–1968) and Chesney Allen (1893–1982) were a musical-comedy duo.

93/ Edward Thomas (1878–1917), Anglo-Welsh poet.

95/ Robert Stephenson Smyth Baden-Powell (1857–1941), British soldier and fouder of the Scouting ovement.

96/ *Piers Plowman*, an allegorical poem written by William Langland circa 1370–90.

98/ "Chants of the Prairies": Walt Whitman, *Leaves of Grass,* "Starting from Paumanok," 3.

98/ Arleigh "31-Knot" Burke (1901–1996), US Navy admiral and chief of naval operations, 1955–61.

98/ "I know a high, round hill": Bill Adams, *Ships and Memories* (Brighton: Teredo Books, 1975).

101/ *Mrs. Dale's Diary* was a BBC radio drama broadcast from 1948 to 1969.

101/ *Zoella Lykes*: A small cargo ship (designated C1-B by the United States Maritime Commission), which served as a troop transport during and just after World War II.

114/ *The Red Balloon (Le Ballon Rouge*, 1956), an award-winning short written and directed by Albert Lamorisse.

115/ *Zurückgewiesen, Schwartz*: Rejected, Black Forest Autobahn.

120/ Rudyard Kipling (1865–1936), British poet and novelist.

120/ H. Rider Haggard (1856–1925), British author of adventure novels, many set in the wilds of the British Empire.

121/ BAR: Browning Automatic Rifle, the US Army's standard-issue light machine gun from 1938 until the early 1960s.

122/ *Apocalypse Now* (1979), directed by Francis Ford Coppolla, stars Marlon Brando, Martin Sheen, and Robert Duvall.

122/ "Ride of the Valkyries" is the name given to the opening of act 3 of Richard Wagner's opera *Die Walküre.*

126/ Montagnard is the French name given to inhabitants of the highlands of central and southern Vietnam.

131/ Dorothy Brett (1883–1977) was the daughter of Lord Asquith, the British prime minister during World War I.

131/ Georgia O'Keefe (1887–1986), an American painter.

133/ Tom Mix (1880–1940), Western movie star known as "King of the Cowboys," with 291 film credits.

134/ "Here, on this little ranch": *In The Modern Tradition: Backgrounds of Modern Literature*, edited by Richard Ellmann and Charles Feidelson, Jr. (New York: Oxford University Press, 1965), 416–23.

135/ Witter Bynner (1881–1968), poet, philanthropist, and friend and travelling companion of Lawrence.

140/ "and crown thy good": "America the Beautiful" (1910), lyrics by Katherine Lee Bates (1859–1929), music by Samuel A. Ward (1847–1903).

140/ Gloria Steinem (b. 1934) and Betty Friedan (1921–2006) are American feminists, activists, and authors.

140/ Barkis and Peggotty: characters in Charles Dickens's serialized novel *David Copperfield* (1849–50).

140/ William S. Burroughs (1914–1997), Harvard-educated Beat Generation novelist whose works included *Junkie* (1953) and *Naked Lunch* (1959).

141/ Franz Léhar (1870–1948), Austro-Hungarian composer best known for his operetta *Die lustige Witwe* (The Merry Widow, 1905).

141/ *Hair: The American Tribal Love-Rock Musical* (1967), with book and lyrics by James Rado and Gerome Ragni and music by Galt MacDermot, is considered the first rock opera.

143/ Reies Lopez Tijerina (1926–2015), itinerant preacher and Chicano activist.

143/ "one of the most unjust": Ulysses S. Grant, *Personal Memoirs of U. S. Grant* (New York: 1886), ch. 3. Grant (1822–1885) was the Union's commanding general during the Civil War and president of the United States (1869–77).

143/ Henry David Thoreau (1817–1862), American transcendentalist poet and philosopher.

143/ The Treaty of Guadeloupe Hidalgo ending the Mexican-American War (1846–48) confirmed the US annexation of Texas and Mexico ceded the territory of what are now California, Nevada, Utah, New Mexico, most of Arizona, and parts of Wyoming, Nebraska, Oklahoma to the US.

143/ Alianza Federal de Pueblos Libres (The Alliance of Free Pueblos), officially Alianza Federal de Mercedes (Federal Land Grant Alliance), was also known as the Alianza de Pubelos y Pobladores (The Alliance of Towns and Settlers).

144/ Horatius: Publius Horatius Cocles, a Roman soldier who almost single-handedly deflected an Etruscan assault on Rome in the sixth century BCE.

144/ Elizabeth ("Betita") Sutherland Martínez (b. 1925), Chicana feminist and activist.

144/ Beverly Axelrod (1924–2002), civil rights lawyer particularly known for her work with the Black Panthers and Native Americans.

144/ Pancho Villa, nickname of José Doroteo Arango Arámbula (1878–1923), revolutionary general in the Mexican Revolution (or Mexican Civil War, 1910–20).

144/ Eldridge Cleaver (1935–1998), American writer, activist, and leader of the Black Panthers.

144/ Huey Newton (1942–1989), co-founder of the Black Panthers and scholar implicated in several murders and himself murdered by a member of a Panther splinter group.

145/ Angela Davis (b. 1944), African-American political activist, feminist, and scholar.

147/ Horatio Hornblower: hero of twelve novels by C. S. Forester (1899–1966) that recount his rise from midshipman to admiral of the fleet in the Royal Navy of the Napoleonic Wars.

147/ *From Powder Monkey to Admiral* (1879) is an adventure story by W. H. G. Kingston (1814–1880).

149/ John D. Poindexter (b. 1936), later National Security Advisor in the Reagan Administration (1985–86).

152/ OXford 7: Dial telephones used to have alphanumeric telephone numbers such as these. The first two letters and first digit designated a certain geographic area and were referred to as exchanges.

152/ Edwin Hooper (1909–1986), naval officer and historian.

152/ William J. Morgan (1917–2003), historian at the US Naval Historical Center from 1952 to 2002, and editor of *Naval Documents of the American Revolution.*

154/ "I reject": President Gerald R. Ford, Remarks at Ceremonies Commemorating the Bicentennial of the United States Navy, October 9, 1975.

158/ James L. Holloway, III (b. 1922), naval aviator and chief of naval operations, 1974–78.

160/ Down Easter was the name given to square-rigged ships built in Maine—down wind and east of Boston—between the late 1860s and early 1900s.

163/ Norman Brouwer (b. 1938), author of *The International Register of Historic Ships*, first published in 1985, was the librarian and curator of ships at the South Street Seaport Museum.

163/ "We were told" by the Military Sealift Command, John Arens's employer.

163/ ARA: Armada de la República Argentina.

166/ CB: Companion of the Order of Bath, the fourth ranking order of chivalry in the British honors system. Appointments are made for "the performance of public duties [that] have merited … royal favour." CBE: Commander of the Most Excellent Order of the British Empire, the juniormost order of chivalry.

167/ RRS: Royal Research Ship.

168/ Receiver of Wreck: a UK official responsible for processing "reports of wreck, in the interest of both salvor and owner. This involves researching ownership, liaising with finder and owner, and other interested parties such as archaeologists and museums."

168/ *Cutty Sark*: British tea clipper of 1869 now preserved at Greenwich, England, and namesake of the blended Scotch whisky.

169/ HMS *Victory*: British first-rate ship-of-the-line launced in 1769. Lord Nelson's flagship at the battle of Trafalgar, she is preserved at Portsmouth Historic Dockyard.

169/ OBE: Officer of the Most Excellent Order of the British Empire.

171/ Clive Cussler (b. 1931), adventure novelist and nautical archaeologist.

171/ John Paul Jones (1747–1792), Scottish-born American naval hero of the American Revolution who in September 1779 lost his ship, the *Bonhomme Richard,* in a victory over the HMS *Serapis*, which he captured.

172/ Harold "Doc" Edgerton (1903–1990) was an electrical engineer who worked on strobe photography, underwater photographic equipment, and sonar.

172/ *True Grit*: Charles Portis's 1968 novel was made into a movie the next year and earned John Wayne an Academy Award for best actor for his portrayal of Rooster Cogburn.

178/ Shalom Steinbach: The audio interview is available at the website of the US Holocaust Memorial Museum, http://collections.ushmm.org/search/catalog/irn502037. Opened in 1933, the concentration camp at Dachau, sixteen miles north of Munich, was originally intended for political prisoners.

178/ *Cap Arcona:* A passenger ship built for the Hamburg-South America Line, during the war, the *Cap Arcona* was used as an accommodation ship, for evacuating soldiers and civilians from East Prussia, and finally as a prison ship in Lübeck. She was sunk one day before German's unconditional surrender.

179/ WESTLANT: Western Atlantic, NATO's description of North American waters.

179/ "How much": John Masters, *Bugles and a Tiger* (London: Corgi, 1973).

181/ Oliver Cromwell (1599–1658), Lord Protector of the Commonwealth of England, Scotland, and Ireland, after the execution of Charles I for treason.

181/ Rump Parliament: those members of Parliament who remained after those opposed to the king's execution had been purged.

182/ "that a man must act": Masters, *Bugles and a Tiger*.

182/ William Thompson, first public affairs specialist in the Navy to reach flag rank.

182/ Jeremy M. Boorda (1939–1996), first CNO to have risen to the post having entered the navy as an enlisted man.

182/ CIC: Combat Information Center, a warship's tactical center where information is processed.

183/ John Duncan Bulkeley (1911–1996), vice admiral, awarded Medal of Honor for actions in the Pacific during World War II.

183/ James Stockdale (1923–2005), naval aviator, eight-year POW in Vietnam (for which he received the Medal of Honor), and vice presidential candidate in 1992.

185/ "We'll be a Welcome in the Hillside": Song by Mai Jones (1899–1960), first performed at the National Eisteddfod (festival) in 1924.

185/ "Men of Harlech": Welsh folk song said to recount a fifteenth-century siege, though it was not first published until 1794.

185/ "Softly as I Leave You": Italian song, "Piano" (1960) by Giorgio Calabrese (b. 1929) and Antonio DeVita (1932–1998), and translated by Hal Shaper (1961). It has been sung by Frank Sinatra, Bobby Darrin, and many others.

188/ Berrigan brothers: Roman Catholic priests and peace activists Daniel Berrigan (b. 1921) and Philip Berrigan (1923–2002).

188/ "I have defined good": Bernard Rostker, *Depleted Uranium: A Case Study of Good and Evil* (Santa Monica: RAND, 2002), p. 2; http://www.rand.org/content/dam/rand/pubs/papers/2009/P8066.pdf.

189/ Stephen Joseph, MD, Assistant Secretary of Defense for Health Affairs.

189/ Col. Eric Daxon MD, one of the investigating physicians.

189/ Lt. Gen. Dale Vesser, Rostker's deputy.

189/ Gen. H. Norman Schwartzkopf, Jr. (1934–2012), Commander-in-Chief, United States Central Command, who led the allied coalition forces in the Persian Gulf War.

189/ Gen. Colin L. Powell (b. 1937), Chairman of the Joint Chiefs of Staff under President George H. W. Bush, and Secretary of State under President George W. Bush.

189/ Lt. Gen. James R. Clapper, Jr. (b. 1941), US Air Force. As director of the National Geospatial Intelligence Agency (2001–2006), he was my last boss.

194/ Santiago de Compostela: The capital of Galicia, Spain, and since the ninth century the site of a shrine to St. James the Apostle (Santiago) and the terminus of the Camino de Santiago, a pilgrimage route across northern Spain.

194/ *Botafumeiro*: A censer hung from the dome of the Cathedral of Santiago de Compostela.

195/ Jean-Paul Sartre (1905–1980), French philosopher and playwright. *Reflexions sur la question juive* (1944) was translated into English as *Anti-Semite and Jew* (1948).

196/ Stephen Hawking (b. 1942), British theoretical physicist and cosmologist best known for his book *A Brief History of Time* (1992).

196/ Joseph Campbell (1904–87), American mythologist.

197/ Shema: The *Shema Yisrael* is the Jewish confession of faith.

197/ Emile Mâle (1862–1954), French medieval historian and iconography expert.

198/ Based on the 1848 novel of the same name by Alexandre Dumas, fils, *Camille* (1936) starred Greta Garbo as a woman of low birth whose beauty gives her entrée into high society, and who dies of tuberculosis.

199/ Jutland was the site of the largest naval battle of World War I, May 31–June 1, 1916.

199/ Aleksandr Solzhenitsyn (1918–2008), Soviet novelist, dissident, and Nobel Prize winner whose works include *The Gulag Archipelago* (1958–68), *One Day in the Life of Ivan Denisovich* (1962), and *Cancer Ward* (1968).

199/ OSB: Order of Saint Benedict (ca. 480–543), who is considered the founder of western Christian monasticism. Merton's *New Seeds of Contemplation* was published in 1962.

203/ R. S. Thomas (1913–2000), Welsh-born Anglican priest and poet. "The Bright Field," in *Collected Poems, 1945–1990* (London: Dent, 1993), 302.

208/ Peter Lorre (1904–1964), Hungarian-born actor whose film debut was as Hans Beckert in Fritz Lang's *M* (1931).

209/ Franz Lehár (1870–1948), Austro-Hungarian composer best known for his operetta *Die lustige Witwe* (The Merry Widow, 1905).

209/ Alecto: one of the Furies in Greek mythology.

210/ Penelope Fitzgerald (1916–2000), English novelist and Booker Prize winner; the quote is from her novel *Offshore* (1979).

212/ "To me, O Lord": Helen Corke, *Songs of Autumn* (Austin: University of Texas Press, 1960).